AUTHOR'S PREFACE

My earliest memories of football include a visit to Seedhill in season 19... ... I was just twelve years old at the time, and staying during school holidays with my grandparents at nearby Colne. Sadly, Nelson's opponents – whose name eludes me but who played in white shirts and dark shorts – managed to frustrate the best efforts of Nelson's fair-haired inside-forward, Arthur Woodcock, as I looked on from behind the goals, hoping for a successful strike from my much admired 'Uncle Arthur'.

It was not until many years later that I came to realise that Nelson F.C. had once been a Football League club, and I was grateful to Tony Brown of Soccerdata Publications, for sharing my enthusiasm for the concept of a book to chronicle the club's decade of League membership, told mainly through the careers of the 166 players who made a first team appearance between 1921–31.

Given the length of time since Nelson enjoyed membership of the Football League, and the wealth of detail required for each player's entry, it would be surprising if the odd error has not crept in, and for any that have, I apologise in advance. Researches into our national game are ongoing, and amplification of information on any of the players who have qualified for inclusion in this book will be warmly welcomed. I can be contacted via the publisher.

Garth Dykes
Leicester
October 2009.

ACKNOWLEDGEMENTS

Four old friends, and one new one, are all most sincerely thanked for their kindness and help during the preparation of this book. My new friend, Bernard Metcalfe of Nelson, has greatly enriched the pages of this book thanks to his regular reports, following visits to Nelson Library, responding with unfailing enthusiasm to my many queries. My old friends, Michael Braham, Jim Creasy, Mike Davage and Mike Jackman have, as ever, been generous with their time and knowledge. I would also like to thank Peter Holme, Research Officer at the Football Museum at Preston, for access to their records, and my gratitude to Andy Cowie of Colorsport for his help with the supply of many excellent photographs. My gratitude also to Alyson Walker of the Nelson Community History Library, and to the following individuals for their kind assistance: Jean Ingham, David W. Marshall, Jack Lord, Hilary M. Carter, Peter Caine, Robert W. Reid of Partick Thistle FC, Harry C. Manning and Gary Broughton.

Nelson FC 1922-23

Football League Division Three (North) Champions

Players only: Standing, left to right: C Rigg, E Braidwood, J Birds, D Wilson, JE Broadhead. Seated: SJ Hoad, R Lilley, MJ McCulloch, J Eddleston, A Wolstenholme, R Hutchinson.

NELSON FC

The town of Nelson was sparsely populated in the year 1881, but enthusiasm for football quickly took root. Although early records of the local club have been lost in the mists of antiquity, dates and details emerged when, eight years later, they became founder members of the Lancashire League, and finished in fourth place in their first season. One of the early founders of the club was Mr Joe Snowden, who, despite taking no active part in the management of the club in his later years, took a very keen interest up to the time of his death in the late 1920s.

The story might have ended before the dawn of the twentieth century, when the first of many struggling days saw the club disband in mid-season 1898-99, following a suspension imposed by the Football Association. Happily, the club was re-born during the close season and their faltering path continued, initially as members of the North East Lancashire Combination.

Despite days of struggle, by 1905, the team moved to their new ground, Seedhill. Although average wages for a professional footballer in those far off days were half-a-crown a week (equivalent to twelve and a half pence in today's money), many were the times when Committee members had to go round with the hat to publicans and tradesmen on a Friday night to raise money to convey the team to an away match. It is also on record that a creditor put the bailiffs in. The only saleable asset was the old grandstand, but a kindly benefactor, Mr Joseph Wooliscroft, bought the stand and gave it back to the Nelson club. It was subsequently dismantled and sold to Barnoldswick Town in 1923.

For several seasons prior to the First World War, Nelson had a good team. In season 1910-11 they fielded several players who had plenty of experience of good-class football before joining the Seedhill ranks. These included Frank Corvan, Johnny Low, "Fran" Burton and "Cobbler" Hodgkinson, a dashing, free-scoring centre-forward. At that time, Colne were in the same league as Nelson, and the "Derby" matches featured local rivalry at its most intense. In two matches during the season, one a Combination fixture and one a Cup-tie, receipts on each occasion were close to £100 – a goodly sum, considering that the price of admission was only 4d.

Nelson finished third in the Lancashire Combination in 1912-13, but, for the second time in their history, they ceased to function after completing a season of wartime football in the Supplementary Competitions of 1915-16. After a lapse of over four years, football was resumed. A new Management Committee succeeded in clearing debts of over £1,500, and commenced operations in a new sphere. Having, for a lengthy period, been members of the Lancashire Combination, they gained admission to the Central League, an improvement in status as the league comprised mainly of the reserve teams of Football League clubs.

The 1919-20 season featured many returning soldiers. Outside-right J. Rigby had played for four years with the 1/2nd East Lancashire Field Ambulance team and also assisted the Brussels Racing Club. Wing-half Edgar Jacques had spent over two years as a prisoner of war, happily being released on his birthday in November 1918. Another returning soldier, H. Broadley, whose only pre-war experience was obtained in the Burnley Sunday School League, nevertheless started by scoring both goals in a 2–1 win against Everton Reserves at Seedhill on the opening day. He went on to score in each of his first nine matches, scoring 12 of the team's first 22 goals.

Other players signed after the reconstruction included Sam Wadsworth and Harry Hargreaves. Both were later sold for substantial fees to other clubs. Wadsworth joined Huddersfield Town in March 1921 for a fee of £1,600. He went on to win nine England caps, three consecutive Football League championships, and the FA Cup in 1922. Harry Hargreaves went on to star with Wolverhampton Wanderers, Tottenham Hotspur and Burnley.

After just one more season of Central League football, Nelson gained admittance to the newly formed Northern Section of the Third Division. League status brought an upsurge in interest and greatly increased "gates" were attracted to Seedhill. Receipts amounting to £569 were taken from the visit of Accrington Stanley on October 15th, 1921. With a shrewd player-manager in David Wilson, the former Scottish international, rapid progress was made. In their second season as a Football League club, Nelson won the championship of the Third Division North. Every position in the team was capably filled, and there were efficient reserves available in the case of emergencies.

Arguably the best team that Nelson ever had lined up as follows: Birds; Lilley, Rigg; D. Wilson, Braidwood, Broadhead; Hoad, Wolstenholme, Eddleston, McCulloch and Hutchinson.

In preparation for life in Division Two, a close season tour of Spain was undertaken. Six matches were played, the outstanding result being a 4–2 victory against Real Madrid. During the same close season the Directors proceeded with an ambitious ground improvement and extension scheme. A new stand was erected on the Carr Road side of the ground, bringing the capacity to 25,000. The playing pitch was considerably enlarged, adding a further 2,000 square yards to the surface. A crowd of approximately 12,000 attended the season's opener against Clapton Orient at Seedhill and a 1–1 draw ensued. A pattern of draws at home and defeats away was halted when Stoke were beaten 2–0 at Seedhill on 29th October, the side's first win in nine matches. Even at this early stage, it was apparent that the team were in for a difficult season and although faint hopes survived throughout, the bitter disappointment of relegation was finally sealed on the last day of the season. This despite a 3–1 home win against the season's champions, Leeds United. Results elsewhere condemned Nelson to the dreaded drop, after just one season in the Second Division.

During the close season, player-manager David Wilson made several new signings, and a large number of promising amateurs from local football were added to the playing staff. Chief interest was focused on Ellerington and W. Bottrill from Middlesbrough, and O'Beirne, the former Burnley inside-left. Among the departed were old

Player-manager David Wilson

favourites Black and McCullouch, and former player Jacques was appointed assistant trainer and groundsman. The team was considered a stronger one than that which won promotion two seasons ago, and they came within a whisker of regaining their Second Division status. Spearheaded by Joe Eddleston, who scored 26 League and Cup goals during the campaign, promotion was very much on the cards until the final month of the season, when only two wins were obtained from the final nine matches. Darlington took the title, with Nelson and New Brighton five points adrift. Nelson taking the runners-up position with a better goal average.

The new season commenced in August 1925, and in the final pre-season trial, the Reserves scored four goals in the first twelve minutes, as the first team defence struggled to come to terms with the new off-side rule, which required two players between the attacking player and the goal, rather than the previous requirement of three. A glut of goals was expected, and in this case delivered, as the first team rallied to win 6–4, but it took some time for the side to settle when the serious business began, one win in the first seven matches being anything but promotion form. The Director's bold step in paying a record fee for George Wilson, the Sheffield Wednesday and England international centre-half, was an unqualified success, as his outstanding displays in both defence and attack eventually rallied his colleagues and although the side again ran out of steam in the final weeks of the season, eighth position in the final table was a respectable placing. The team scored 89 League goals, highlights being consecutive 7–0 home wins against Tranmere Rovers and Wigan Borough in December, and the side remained unbeaten at Seedhill until the very last match, when Rochdale spoiled the record with a 3–1 win.

Despite the disappointment of losing leading goal scorer Joe Eddleston in the close season – he refused terms and was transferred to Swindon Town – a worthy replacement was waiting in the wings. Youthful centre-forward Jimmy Hampson improved with every match, and finished his first season in senior football with 25 goals in 37 League and Cup matches. Close season recruitment had been concentrated on the half-back line. Although George Wilson was always a power at centre-half, the flank positions were strengthened by the recruitment of J.W. Baker, the former captain of Leeds United, and R. Mitchell, the former Hull City player. Another key signing was Kenny Sharp, a well-built inside-left from Leicester City, who scored 24 League and Cup goals during the season. An eleven-match unbeaten run that commenced with a 4–0 win against Ashington on 13th September 1926, concluded with a 7–1 thrashing of Crewe Alexandra on 13th November. A 3–2 defeat at Hartlepools ended the sequence, but five of the following six matches were won to take Nelson up to second place in the table. The club was still in contention until Easter, but the now familiar failings returned, and the season ended with a run of six consecutive defeats. Fifth place in the table with 104 League goals scored and 75 conceded might have suggested an enjoyable spectacle overall, but home gates fell to an average of just under 6,000, and the season's workings revealed a loss in excess of £1,000.

Numerous changes were the order of the day as the club prepared for season 1927-28. Mr. P.J. Smith, the secretary-manager departed to Bury. His assistant, Mr E. Crabtree took over secretarial duties. Nine professional players were released. These included Abbott, goalkeeper for the past four seasons, who signed with Luton Town. Fred Broadhurst, the veteran back, signed for Chorley. Keers moved to Boston United and Mitchell to Bristol Rovers. A completely new defence was signed – and considering that the side were to concede a staggering 136 League goals during the season, none of the newcomers exactly covered themselves in glory. Best of the bunch was 35 year-old veteran Joe Halliwell, the former Preston North End and Barnsley right-half, who stayed for two seasons and made 74 League appearances. The season commenced with a 1–4 home defeat by Accrington Stanley at Seedhill and a 1–0 reverse at Rochdale. Four consecutive victories followed, but this was followed by six matches without a win. November saw the side humiliated by Manchester City, who thrashed Nelson 10–2 in the Lancashire Senior Cup, while in the League match at Bradford City, Nelson suffered another humiliating reverse by nine goals to one. The sale of star centre-forward Jimmy Hampson to Blackpool in the previous month had disappointed all the club's supporters, although Bernard Radford proved a capable replacement with 17 goals in 20 League matches, the main failings were in defence. Finishing at the foot of the table, Nelson were re-elected, but their companions in distress, Durham City, who finished in 21st place, were not. Carlisle United being elected as their replacement.

A new manager, Mr Jack English, the old Sheffield United and Preston North End full-back and former Darlington manager was appointed for the start of the 1928-29 season, and practically a clean sweep of the playing staff was made. Only six of the previous season's players

Jimmy Hampson

7

remained and new recruits included J. Metcalfe (Preston North End), G. Kelly (Sunderland), T. Wilkinson (Everton) and H. Ridley (Aldershot). Just one defeat after six matches was followed by six successive defeats, and the yo-yo pattern persisted throughout, away form being particularly dismal. A high scoring encounter at Accrington Stanley (4–4) wound up the season with Nelson in 15th place. Despite a significant increase in average home attendances, the club's directors let it be known that losses were mounting, and that they could not be expected to go on indefinitely finding money to carry the club along.

As the Nelson Supporters' Club looked forward to the new season, they were quoted as saying: "Summer time is quite nice and very welcome to everyone, but to the ordinary football enthusiast the last Saturday in August is the day most looked forward to". A team with four new faces (Fairhurst, Ferrari, McLaughlan and Hedley) opened the season with a 2–2 draw against Southport at Seedhill, but three defeats followed. In each of the first four matches of the season, a new goalkeeper was fielded. Warhurst, Mangham and Botto were followed by Shevlin, who retained the position for all but two matches in the rest of the season. The team scored 51 League goals and conceded 80 and finished in nineteenth place in the table. The customary end-of-season slump was again in evidence, all six of the final League matches ending in defeat. A serious injury to captain George Wilson restricted the veteran centre-half to just twelve matches throughout the campaign, and enforced his retirement in the close season.

With finances again a matter of grave concern, the Supporters' Club centred their efforts on clearing the debt on the new stand as quickly as possible. Their latest novelty offering was a "Good class lead pencil, with the first club's home fixtures printed on in club colours". Local industry was also enlisted, weavers William Uttley & Sons Ltd,

Gerard Kelly

donating a welcome two guineas, in celebration of winning a local cricket competition. The trade depression sadly played havoc with attendances across all Divisions of the Football League, and a season that commenced in a heat wave ended in atrocious playing conditions, heavy snow restricting the attendance at several matches to a figure below 2,000 spectators.

Manager English's new recruits for the 1930-31 season were mainly young and relatively inexperienced players, the only signing with a significant top flight pedigree being Arthur Hawes, the former Norwich City, South Shields, Sunderland, Bradford Park Avenue and Accrington Stanley inside forward. Eight players who had been awarded free transfers were still not fixed up with new clubs by late August. Arthur Bate, one of the newcomers, led the line in the season's opener at Rochdale. In weather more suited to cricket than soccer he marked his debut in the Football League by netting a hat-trick. Sadly, it was not enough to earn a winning bonus as the home side won a thrilling, end-to-end encounter, by five goals to four. Another two goals from Bate and one from Archie Howarth accounted for Darlington in the third match of the season, but a subsequent run of eight League matches without a win left the side well adrift. It seemed ironic that the Nelson Football Club was in such dire straits, while their immediate neighbours, the Nelson Cricket Club, were prospering. The cricket club's results, announced in December 1930, revealed that they had made a profit of £352 on the year. Gate money had totalled £1,328, and members – 1,564 of them – had paid £878. Their was, however, no upturn for Nelson's long suffering football supporters at the turn of the year, as the team were soundly thrashed 8–1 at Southport on New Years' Day, and a six-match winless streak in February and March included another 8–1 reverse, at Carlisle United. Six defeats in succession ended Nelson's worst-ever season.

With a record of just six wins and 19 points from 42 matches, the club was marooned at the foot of the table, eleven points behind Rochdale, fellow applicants for re-election. While Rochdale were re-elected, polling forty votes, Nelson tied with Chester on twenty-seven votes. This necessitated a second ballot, which Chester won by a margin of eight votes. So ended Nelson's up-and-down decade as a Football League club. The highlights of which included the Third Division North championship in 1923, and a season in Division Two that included famous victories against Manchester United at Old Trafford, and against Leeds United, the season's champions, at Seedhill. The summer tour to Spain in 1923 that included victories against Real Madrid and Racing Club Santander was another happy highlight. For three seasons following relegation from Division Two, the team enjoyed a degree of success, finishing runners-up in the Northern Section in 1924-25, eighth in 1925-26 and fifth in 1926-27. The last four seasons, however, saw the side in terminal decline, with two re-election applications, and finishes of fifteenth and nineteenth in between.

Sadly, when World War Two suspended football activities, Nelson had already dropped out of the Lancashire Combination and had been wound up. A new team, Nelson Town, operating from the Seedhill ground, entered the Nelson, Colne and District Amateur League for season 1936-37 and they enjoyed initial success by winning the Amos Nelson Cup. In the following season they joined the Lancashire Amateur League, but their upward progress was halted after just two matches in the West Lancashire League in 1939-40, when the competition was aborted on the outbreak of hostilities. On Tuesday 16th October 1939 a Committee meeting of the Nelson Town club confirmed that, in view of the financial obligations that would be entailed by carrying on, they had reluctantly concluded that it would be unwise to continue. Chairman Mr J. Crabtree adding that any members who had already paid their subscription could apply to have the money refunded.

Harry Hargreaves

Post war soccer was welcomed back to Seedhill in season 1946-47 when another Nelson FC was launched. They took the lead within five minutes of the kick-off in their opener against Rossendale United, but lost 2–1 to a goal scored in the dying moments. Despite unseasonable weather, a crowd of around 5,000 spectators witnessed the match. Nelson's first post war line up was: Bentley; Bannister, Arnold; Sunter, Holmes, Walton; Livesey, Heyes, Hillen, Maudsley, Whalley. A mid table finish was achieved, the team scoring exactly 100 goals, and there was no shortage of goals throughout the early post war years as the team enjoyed great success, winning two Combination championships in 1950 and 1952, and finishing as runners-up in 1948 and 1951. The Combination Cup was also won in successive seasons, 1950 and 1951. As the reserve team were runners-up in Division Two of the Combination in 1948 and 1952, the squad available would doubtless have more than held their own in Third Division football had they managed to gain re-election to the Football League.

The club were runners-up again in the Combination in 1961 but relegation to Division Two followed in 1966, with 121 goals conceded in 42 matches. In 1982-83, Nelson were a founder member of the North West Counties League. Apart from four seasons in the West Lancashire League, the club has continued in membership of the North West Counties League, winning promotion to Division One (now renamed as the Premier Division) in 2006.

The club's last ten-year League record is as follows:

			p	w	d	l	f	a	w	d	l	f	a	pts
1998/1999	First N/W Trains N.W.C. Second Division	13th/19	36	4	6	8	28	32	7	5	6	23	17	44
1999/2000	First N/W Trains N.W.C. Second Division	3rd/18	34	14	0	3	49	12	7	8	2	28	19	71
2000/2001	N.W.C. Second Division	4th/20	38	12	3	4	49	23	9	8	2	40	21	74
2001/2002	N.W.C. Second Division	9th/21	40	11	3	6	43	27	7	6	7	30	36	63
2002/2003	N.W.C. Second Division	7th/18	34	10	2	5	27	17	3	10	4	23	23	51
2003/2004	N.W.C. Second Division	10th/20	38	7	7	5	30	29	7	4	8	25	35	53
2004/2005	Moore & Co. N.W.C. Second Division	6th/19	36	12	3	3	45	24	4	8	6	30	28	59
2005/2006	Moore & Co. N.W.C. Second Division	3rd/19	36	12	1	5	45	25	11	4	3	37	28	74
2006/2007	N.W.C. First Division	20th/22	42	5	4	12	19	40	2	2	17	22	73	27
2007/2008	Vodkat N.W.C. First Division	20th/20	38	3	4	12	22	41	2	4	13	20	49	23
2008/2009	Vodkat N.W.C. Premier Division	17th/22	42	3	8	10	30	43	8	4	9	38	43	45

Another picture of the 1922-23 championship winning team. Standing, left to right: R Lilley (partially obscured), Mr W. Hartley (Chairman), JH Steel, C Rigg, J Birds, E Braidwood, JE Broadhead, MJ McCulloch, SJ Hoad, H Smith (trainer). Front: JR Black, J Eddleston, A Wolstenholme, D Wilson (player-manager), RL Crawshaw, R Hutchinson.

Seedhill in the 1960s

A goalkeeper's lot is not a happy one. Nelson's Harry Abbott looks forward to diving into the mud, 1924

MATCHES TO REMEMBER

THE MANCHESTER UNITED CONNECTION

Nelson and Manchester United have enjoyed rather different success on the football field. Their paths have crossed on a few occasions, firstly when the original Nelson club met United's forerunners Newton Heath in the FA Cup of 1896-1897.

ENGLISH CUP QUALIFYING COMPETITION
Newton Heath 3 Nelson 0
January 1897

This qualifying tie for the English Cup was played at Clayton, before 5000 spectators. Cockshutt started for Nelson, and they were the first to run down, Cartwright showing some prominence with a couple of good kicks in defence of his goal. Then the home side managed to change the mode of attack, but the ground was slippery, and prevented them from getting along. Nelson went down with some nice passes, Cockshutt and Worrall doing good work in getting the ball down. Stafford and Cartwright, however, soon turned them the other way, and then the home left got down, and a free kick was granted, which M'Naught placed nicely in front of goal, and the amateur, Stephenson, placed the ball into the net with his head. After this Nelson attacked, their halves kicking strongly, and by this means their forwards found something in front of them which was by no means easy to get past, Stafford and Cartwright kicking well. The home lot next went down, and Bryant, when standing offside, placed the ball into the net, and no goal was allowed. Half time arrived with Newton Heath leading by one goal to none. Stephenson started the second half, and he gave to Cassidy, who again gave back to Stephenson, and then the ball found its way to Donaldson, who could not do anything with it owing to the close attention of Green, and the ball went over the goal line. The Nelson team ran up, and Cartwright had to do a little bit of manoevering to get the ball out of the way of Worrall and Wilson. He, however, succeeded, and play went towards the forward line, but Bryant was lame, and could not do much. Then a run on the home left saw Donaldson send across a lovely centre, and Bryant met it with his head, and landed the ball safely past M'Owen into the net. Nelson afterwards made several good runs, but their forwards could not make any impression on the home defence, which was in its usual good condition. Another attack on the Nelson goal saw Jenkyns, the heavyweight, tripped about half a dozen yards from the goal, a trip which brought him down heavily to the ground. The free kick was taken by Stafford, and he placed it nicely, for somebody's head to put the ball into the net, the left wing doing the trick and making the score three goals.
Manchester Courier January 4 1897

and the same match as seen by the Athletic News:

For the winners Barrett cleared some good shots, and he had a bit of a chance of showing what he could do for once, as Errentz was off. The halves were not quite so conspicuous as usual, M'Naught being the pick. Stevenson was brought into the vacant place in the front rank, going centre, and Cassidy inside right. The first named made a fair show, but Cassidy was not suited either by his position or by the hard ground. Donaldson and Bryant were the best, while Gillespie was a bit off, but all of them made many mistakes. Newton Heath will now have to play Blackpool, at Clayton, for the right of way into the competition proper, and remembering Blackpool's good form here the other week they have little in hand - on paper at any rate. It should be a most interesting meeting.

Newton Heath spent most of their Football League career in the Second Division, and it was 1906-07 before the re-formed club, Manchester United, first played in Division One. They finished bottom in 1921-22 and spend three seasons in Division Two, one of them coinciding with Nelson's visit. The clubs met at Old Trafford in March 1924:

NELSON WIN FIRST AWAY GAME
Manchester United 0, Nelson 1
March 8, 1924

The first dangerous movement came from the United right wing, Spence finishing a neat round of passing with a high backward centre, which went over to M'Pherson. The outside-left got the ball to Grimwood, but the latter was tackled by Braidwood in the act of shooting, and his effort lost strength as a consequence. Strong work by Rigg and Braidwood set the visitors going, and Newnes was accurate in his pass to Higginbotham, but offside pulled up Caulfield. The turf was greasy, and the men found it difficult to turn. The most dangerous move so far seen now came from Caulfield, who broke clear on the right wing, and cutting inside found himself not more than 12 yards from Steward. He drove at the net, but the custodian was in the line of flight and beat down the ball.

Caulfield put in a beautiful bit of work, beating Hilditch twice before he centred well in front of Steward. The Nelson forwards were not able to take advantage of the opportunity, and play swung back in the visitors' half, Abbott meeting with both fists under the bar a very fine drive from Grimwood. In the next few minutes M'Pherson and Kennedy made desperate efforts to break through the Nelson defence without success, and then Lochhead, breaking away from the centre line, dribbled round both Braidwood and Lilley, creating an opening for Mann, who failed to take advantage. A few minutes later a fine effort by Lochhead and M'Pherson again left the ball with Mann, but the inside right was not happy in front of goal. With 19 minutes gone a well-worked Nelson attack was smartly finished by CRAWSHAW, who was quick to bring the ball to his foot and drove low for the corner of the net. The shot completely beat Seward. Kennedy and Lochhead were playing clever football, but the United forwards could do nothing right in front of goal. Although not so often on the attack, the Nelson forwards were decidedly business-like in their methods when on the ball. One of the best efforts of the game came from Grimwood. Lilley kicked it out, and immediately afterwards M'Pherson, working close in, drove against the side of the post from short range.

Again M'Pherson came into the picture. His speed carries him past Lilley, but his final effort, a low cross shot on the run, was quite easily saved by Abbott. A perfect centre by Spence was cleared by the Nelson defenders, but the visiting forwards were, so far, very little in evidence.

12

Lochhead broke right through in the centre; keeping the ball under control in remarkable style, and finally turning it over to M'Pherson as the latter dashed up on the left. M'Pherson at short range endeavoured to shoot, but only half-hit the ball, which skidded off his foot yards wide of the post. Spence forced a corner kick and placed it well. Following the goal-mouth scrimmage Lochhead drove in a furious shot, which Abbott turned away in great style. The United for a long time did all the attacking, the game being very one-sided. A long shot by Higginbotham was an excellent effort, and Steward had to concede a corner as he leaped to reach it.

In the opening minutes of the second half a low drive by Kennedy passed just outside the foot of the post. The home forwards commenced with great energy, but no one could get a shot at Abbott, and Eddleston broke into the United half, Moore breaking up the attack. Lochhead looked like going through just after this, but lost control of the ball in the goalmouth. A fast cross-drive from Spence just passed wide of the foot of the far post. Following a corner kick, Grimwood tried a long shot, but was wide of the mark. The Nelson half-backs were working might and main, and generally the visitors' defence was excellent. A swinging kick across the ground from M'Pherson left Spence with a chance, but his shot was ill-directed. Twice Humphrey and Crawshaw, the Nelson left-wing pair, broke into the Manchester half, but Radford on each occasion tackled well, and when Caulfield broke away with a pass from Newnes, Radford cleared his centre. A centre by M'Pherson was promptly cleared and when Abbott fisted out a high dropping ball from Spence Kennedy flashed in and hurt himself in making a great effort to head the ball into the corner of the net, the ball just passing outside the post. Kennedy resumed, and immediately afterwards there came a strong effort by the Nelson forwards, Humphrey swinging the ball over from the left-wing and Caulfield driving wide of the goal. Eddleston twice went very near to breaking through on his own, and Crawshaw was just too high with another short-range effort. Mann was right through on his own, but with only Abbott to beat he drove wide of the post. Nelson were fighting with great pluck, but the home team were giving a poor exhibition. The home forwards continued to press, and nearly all the play was in the Nelson half. Once Abbott fisted away a high ball from Spence after a shot by Kennedy had sped outside the post.
Nelson Leader

The Athletic News reported the same game as follows:

NELSON'S HONOUR
Unhappy finish at Old Trafford

Manchester United, with a reorganised forward line, were beaten at home on Saturday because they had not a marksman in their attack. For three-parts of the game the ball was in the Nelson half, but so well did the visiting defence play that the one goal seen in the game won the match. This was scored by CRAWSHAW after nineteen minutes play.

Two minutes from the finish Eddleston was going through in the centre with Radford on his heels. The United back was beaten, but brought down his opponent. The referee consulted the lineman, and sent Radford off the field. Eddleston was carried off injured.

The great counter attraction in the City reduced the attendance to just under 14,000 people, who saw a very poor game, which had few attractive incidents. The honours went to the Nelson defence. Lilley and Rigg protected Abbott so well that, despite the great pressure brought to bear by the home forwards, the visiting custodian was rarely tested.

Nelson had a young recruit in Wilson at left half-back, and he acquitted himself quite well. Braidwood at centre half-back was a great worker in the Nelson defence. The visiting forwards were little in the picture, but when on the move they were quite businesslike in their methods. Caulfield, at outside right, and Eddleston, at centre forward, worrying the Manchester defence not a little.

Newnes played a strong game in the Nelson half-back line, and one can have nothing but praise for the resolute defence of the visiting side. Once they had gained the lead they concentrated on defence, and time after time packed their own goal in successful endeavour to meet the desperate efforts of the United forwards.

The home defence had but little serious work to do, their half-backs having a tight grip on the visiting forward line. Lochhead, tried at centre-forward for the first time this season, was very clever, but inclined to play too close a game, and Kennedy was the best United inside forward. M'Pherson, at outside left, was weak, but Spence was strong and accurate in his centres.
Athletic News March 10 1924

You will notice the reference to "a young recruit Wilson at left-half" in the Athletic News report. This was in fact player-manager Dave Wilson, then nearly 40 years of age. The Nelson Leader assumed Joe Eddleston had taken delight in misleading the Manchester reporters!

Moving on some 80 years, the disenchantment of a group of Manchester United supporters with the Glazer take-over of the club, plus the general commercialisation of Premiership football, led to the formation in 2005 of a new club, FC United of Manchester. Starting near the bottom of the non-League pyramid, they are currently clawing their way up towards the Conference and the Football League. The new club's path crossed with Nelson in 2005-06. Having lost 0-6 in the away game the Nelson fans hoped for better things in the return. The result, alas (from a Nelson viewpoint), was 0-8.

Back to the 1920s for the final match report. Nelson won the Division Three (North) championship in 1923 with two games to spare:

NELSON WIN THE CHAMPIONSHIP

Nelson 2, Wrexham 0
April 24th 1923 (from the Nelson Leader)

Unparalled scenes were witnessed on the Nelson ground on Tuesday evening, when Nelson played their return game with Wrexham. If Nelson won, their position as champions was assured, and consequently the match excited the greatest interest. The setting could not have been more fitting. The night was perfect, and one of the largest crowds of the season assembled. A great number went straight from the mill to the field without tea, motor charabancs conveying parties from the out of way places of the town. One or two mills stopped a little earlier so that the workpeople could get down in time, and when the teams turned out - preceded by a jazz band - the scene was a most animated one. The grandstand was packed, and in the crowd one could see standing one or two ex-mayors from Burnley, and legislators and managers from other clubs. Tom Maley, of Bradford, was amongst the company, and he had a double interest, for Bradford had just an outside chance if Nelson failed. One or two of the Bradford players were also present, to say nothing of Tom Boyle and other Burnley players. Blue and white rosettes were freely worn by the Nelson supporters, and the whole scene lent itself to an historic occasion.

Nelson were still without Wilson and Steele, and there was a fear that the excitement of the game might have its effect on the play of the Nelsonians. The crows apparently suffered more from nerves than the players, for the latter immediately got into their stride, and began to exert pressure on the visitors goal. The ball was lively and passes sometimes went astray, but McCulloch soon came into prominence by the dexterity with which he got the ball under control and fed Wolstenholme. His pass to Hoad was too strong, and the ball went out of play, but the outside right missed a chance of centering immediately afterwards. Rigg made a characteristically cool clearance when the visitors right wing got away, and Hutchinson centred for Eddleston to test Godding with a capital shot which he cleared well. Crawshaw raced away once to drive the ball right across goal and just outside the post, Godding being helpless. After 11 minutes Nelson scored a fine goal. Hutchinson got possession of the ball from a goal kick, and, outpacing Regan and Holmes, he centered beautifully for **Crawshaw** to drive home a low shot.

There was no mistaking the superiority of the Nelson side at this stage, for it was only on rare occasions that Wrexham got away, Black once conceding a corner which was easily cleared. Godding, at the other end, was constantly in action, saving cleverly a header from Crawshaw, whilst he made a brilliant clearance from Eddleston. The Nelson centre forward ran away from all opposition, but when he was in the penalty area Godding ran out, covered Eddleston's view, and held a terrific shot from a few yards range. A second time Eddleston was racing through, but this time he was fouled just outside the penalty area, but Holmes got his foot to Braidwood's shot and cleared. Crawshaw made another great effort to score, but his shot rolled right across the face of goal and out at the post. Jones was the best forward on the visitors side, and once clever work by him almost caused the downfall of the home goal, Birds catching his centre and clearing. Rigg was vociferously applauded for the way in which he tricked Burton and Cotton. A corner for Wrexham in the last minute of the first half was easily cleared.

Nelson again took command of the game in the second half, Godding fisting away from Hoad in the first few minutes, while Wolstenholme had hard luck with a great shot which laid Holmes out. Eddleston shot yards wide when splendidly placed in the penalty area, and Crawshaw was twice dispossessed as he attempted to break through. McCulloch twice sent in long dropping shots which Godding safely caught, and try as they would Nelson could not break down a very fine defence. On the other hand, the visitors forwards were well held on the whole, but once Rigg sent the crowd into great enthusiasm by a magnificent clearance. Fears of a breakaway and an equaliser were silenced at the end of 21 minutes play, for **Eddleston** took advantage of a clever pass from Crawshaw to score a second goal. Hats and caps were thrown into the air, and a scene of great enthusiasm followed. With the game well in hand, Nelson proceeded to play skilful football, and Wolstenholme had decidedly hard lines once when he lifted the ball over Godding's head as he advanced, but it went a yard or so outside the post. Nelson won by 2 goals to nil.

REMARKABLE ENTHUSIASM. TRIUMPHAL STREET PROCESSION.

Immediately the game was over, the crowd surged across the field, and it was with difficulty the Nelson players were able to reach the shelter of the pavilion. They were not allowed to remain there long, for in response to calls of the crowd, the players had to come on to the balcony and submit to the applause of the thousands who were assembled. It was a wonderful spectacle and one which will not readily be forgotten by those privileged to see it. Short speeches were made by Mr W Hartley (Chairman of the Directors), Dave Wilson, who had a particularly cordial reception, Mr J Wooliscroft, and 'Mick' McCulloch. It was impossible to catch all that was said, but so long as the players were on view that was the only thing that mattered. Mr W Hartley expressed his admiration for the team, which had reached the ambition they set out for. It had been a trying time for the directors, and they could now feel happy. It was now up to the public of Nelson to support them. He appealed to the gentlemen in the town to come forward with their aid and give them financial support. It was needed so that they could thoroughly equip their ground and make it suitable for holding large crowds. Dave Wilson said he was the happiest man in Nelson that night. Nelson had made history and reached its ambition. He was proud of the achievement, because he could say with some pride that he had taken part in it. There were not a better set of fellows in the whole country than the Nelson players, both on and off the field. Referring to next season, Mr Wilson said that enthusiasm ran high that night. He hoped it would be maintained throughout next season. By the opening of the new campaign he hoped the new stand would be ready. They wanted many willing workers, and he trusted that everybody who loved football in the town would help them on. If the public would only support them and provide the funds, he could assure them that they would find that their efforts would be rewarded by a good team, worthy of their place in the new company. Subsequently the players were given an enthusiastic triumphal procession throughout the town, the streets being crowded with spectators. Two of the old veterans, Mr J Snowden and Mr J Hopkinson ("Boxer"), were given prominent places in the procession, and both looked supremely happy at the consummation of the season's work.

1925-26. Standing: PJ Smith (secretary-manager), Ted Broadhead, Fred Broadhurst, Jack Newnes, Henry Abbot, Clem Rigg, Bert Smith (Trainer). Seated: Fred Laycock, Edward Earle, Joe Eddleston, George Wilson (captain), Walter Bottrill, James Hampson, Ambrose Harris

1926-27. Standing: Jacques (trainer), Hoad, White, Broadhurst, Mace, Sharp, Rigg, Stevenson, Pearson. Seated: Bailey, Hampson, Wilson, Bedford

1928-29. Standing: Bert Tullock (trainer), D Suttie, E Ferguson, G Kelly, D Fawcett, J Brooks, J Buchanan, P Lewis (assistant trainer). Seated: J Metcalfe, B Radford, G Wilson, JA Halliwell, H Ridley.

NOTES ON THE TEXT

For each player I have attempted to provide the following information: full names, recognised playing position, height and weight, date and place of birth, and date and place of death. It should be mentioned here that the dates of birth and death of some players have been culled from registers that only record such events in three-month periods. Hence the use – for instance – of 'January quarter 1923' – denotes a span of January/February/March of that year. Also included are each player's Nelson debut, full career and biographical details, and a breakdown of appearances made and goals scored. Every player who appeared in a Football League match or an FA Cup-tie has been included.

ABBREVIATIONS

These have been kept to a minimum and are those in general use in works of this type:

App/s	Appearance/s
cs	close season
gl/s	goal/s
q.v. (quod vide)	denoting a cross reference
FA	The Football Association
FL	The Football League
WW1	The First World War (1919-18)
WW2	The Second World War (1939–45)

ABBOTT, Henry 'Harry'

Goalkeeper
5' 9 ½"   12st 7lbs
Born: Preston, July quarter 1897
Died: Preston, April quarter 1968
Career: Lancaster Town 1914. Portsmouth May 1922. NELSON March 1923, fee £15. Luton Town July 1927. Exeter City (trial) August 1929. Lancaster Town September 1929. Rochdale August 1931. Wigan Athletic July 1932.
Debut v Walsall (h) 28.4.23, won 3–0

Signed from Portsmouth towards the close of the 1922-23 promotion season, highly competent goalkeeper Harry Abbott took over from Joe Birds for the two concluding matches. In the following term he quickly established himself as first choice and was rarely absent for four seasons, enjoying a run of 89 consecutive League appearances between 29th March 1924 and 17th April 1926. At the outset of his career his form in a local medal competition in his native Preston led to his joining Lancaster Town. In 1914-15, his first season at the Giant Axe, he appeared in every match, assisting his side to the runners-up position in Division Two of the Lancashire Combination. In the 1921-22 season he was a key member of the team who won the championship of the Combination First Division, being one of just two players to figure in every match during the successful campaign. He had in fact completed three seasons in which he was only once out of the side, and that was when he represented the Lancashire Combination against the Central League at Tranmere in April 1921. After departing Seedhill, Abbott spent two seasons with Luton Town, a Third Division South side at that time. His name remains in the Hatters' record books to this day, as he played in the team's record FA Cup victory, a 9–0 demolition of non-League Clapton at Kenilworth Road on 30th November 1927. His final season of League football was an unhappy one. Rochdale finished at the foot of the Third Division Northern Section, having taken only 11 points from 40 League matches, conceding a staggering 135 goals. In 32 League outings the serious overworked Abbott conceded 92 goals, but his understudy, Bert Welch, fared even worse being beaten 43 times in just eight first team outings.

Appearances: FL: 154 apps 0 gls FAC: 7 apps 0 gls
Total: 161 apps 0 gls

ALLEN, Frank

Inside-forward
5' 9"   11st 10lbs
Born: Altofts, Normanton, 5 May 1901
Died: Ravenshead, Nottingham, 30 October 1989
Career: Altofts WRC circa 1919. Castleford Town 1925. Barnsley February 1926. Bangor City August 1928. Clapton Orient February 1929. Southport June 1929. NELSON August 1930. Barrow January 1931. New Brighton August 1933. Le Havre, France, June 1935. Ollerton Colliery August 1937.
Debut v Rochdale (a) 30.8.30, lost 4–5

One of soccer's happy wanderers, who was once described as "An industrious 90-minute trier", former collier Frank Allen spent only five months at Seedhill, departing the sinking ship in mid term of Nelson's final season in the Football League. Equally at home at inside-right or in the middle line his sojourn began in thrilling fashion. In an

afternoon of all-out attack at Rochdale, Nelson's centre-forward Arthur Bate scored a hat-trick on his debut but, despite his sterling efforts, still finished on the losing side. On leaving Seedhill, Allen blossomed out as a very useful wing-half during his two-plus seasons with Barrow, assisting them to ninth place in the Northern Section in 1932-33 and to fifth in 1933-34. In later years he enjoyed a round of golf and was a keen gardener who enjoyed entering flower shows. He died of pneumonia at the age of 88.
Appearances: FL: 14 apps 0 gls FAC: 3 apps 1 gl Total: 17 apps 1 gl

ANDREWS, Harold Edgar Ramsden

Inside-right
5' 9½" 11st 0lbs
Born: Earby, Lancs, 8 June 1897
Died: Daventry, 20 May 1984
Career: St Cuthbert's FC. Burnley 'A' Team. NELSON professional at the age of 17, registered for FL matches August 1921. Bury August 1922. Luton Town April 1923. Rushden Town August 1923. Chorley October 1924. Torquay United July 1926. Exeter City August 1927. Merthyr Town May 1928. Bath City March 1929. Tunbridge Wells Rangers July 1929. Greens Norton FC Committee October 1948.
Debut v Wigan Borough (h) 27.8.21, lost 1–2
Andrews was born at Earby, but left when only a few months old and grew up in Nelson. Mainly a reserve team player throughout his career, he nevertheless scored prolifically at this level and in non-League circles. He scored 40 goals for Rushden Town in 1923-24, and netted 26 Southern League goals for Torquay United in 1926-27. During his spell with Exeter City, he was reported as playing "A dashing game, neglecting no chance of a shot at goal." He was the Grecian's reserve team leading scorer with 37 goals in Southern and Western League matches in 1927-28. His totals included five against Bath City and four against Torquay United and Salisbury City, and he additionally completed a unique hat-trick (all headers) in a 5–3 win against Aberdare Athletic. He was last traced during a one-month trial with Bath City. He scored one against Exeter City reserves in a 5–0 win and had scored five in his first four matches for his new club. Perhaps his lack of senior action was because he was too individualistic, a not untypical match report contained the following: " Andrews scored a fine goal, but he did not link up with other forwards any too well."
Appearances: FL: 8 apps 1 gl Total: 8 apps 1 gl

BAILEY, Frank

Right-half
5' 7" 10st 6lbs
Born: Burnley, 2 August 1907
Died: Burnley, April quarter 1969
Career: Knowlewood FC. Burnley amateur June 1924. NELSON amateur March, professional October 1926 to January 1928. Great Harwood cs 1929. Lancaster Town July 1930. Rossendale United March 1931. Morecambe August 1934.
Debut v Tranmere Rovers (a) 1.5.26, lost 2–4
Frank Bailey's selections for first team duty could almost be considered an afterthought. He made his debut in the last match of season 1925-26, and his next three appearances came in the final three matches of the following season. Although the side finished in fifth place in the league they ran out of steam in the final run-in, taking only one point from the final seven League matches. Considered a player of great promise on arrival at Seedhill, Bailey failed to rise above reserve team level but subsequently captained Great Harwood and enjoyed a successful career in Lancashire Combination football.
Appearances: FL: 4 apps 0 gls Total: 4 apps 0 gls

BAIRD, Richard

Outside-right
Born: Nelson, 20 February 1892
Died: Nelson, 27 February 1977
Career: NELSON August 1920. Bacup Borough August 1921. Rossendale United July 1921. NELSON January 1922. Chorley May 1922. Rossendale United. Great Harwood September 1923. Colne Carltons FC. Colne Town August 1925.
Debut v Hartlepools United (a) 28.1.22, lost 1- 6
Richard Baird scored twice for Nelson in Central League matches against Stalybridge Celtic and Tranmere Rovers in season 1920-21, but when Nelson commenced in League football in the following term, Baird had departed and was assisting Rossendale United. Recalled to Seedhill in mid season, he was followed, two days later, by Syd Hoad the amateur international outside-right. It was Hoad who subsequently dominated the position and Baird departed after the briefest of stays. Joining Chorley, he assisted them, for the

second time since the war, to win the championship of the Lancashire Combination.
Appearances: FL: 2 apps 0 gls Total: 2 apps 0 gls

BAKER, James William 'Jim'

Wing-half 5' 9" 12st 7lbs
Born: Ilkeston, 15 November 1891
Died: Leeds, 13 December1966
Career: Eastwood Rangers. Ilkeston Town. Derby County amateur December 1910. Portsmouth September 1912. Hartlepools United July1912. Huddersfield Town May 1914. Leeds United May 1920. NELSON June1926, fee £125. Colne Valley.
Debut v Wigan Borough (a) 28.8.26, lost 1–2
Jim Baker arrived at Seedhill with a big reputation, possessing long and varied experience with Huddersfield Town and Leeds United. He was captain of Leeds when they won the championship of the Second Division in season 1923-24. One of a trio of brothers who played League football, Aaron also assisted Leeds United before joining Sheffield Wednesday. Alf appeared in over 350 first team matches for Arsenal between 1919 and 1931, won one England cap and was an FA Cup winner in 1930. Prior to joining the Seedhill ranks, Jim appeared in exactly 200 League matches for Leeds United. Affectionately dubbed "Th'owd War Horse", his absence from the team in late season effectively ended the club's promotion push. One match report during the season gave a clear insight to his value to the side: "Baker was the embodiment of efficiency and, as usual, extracted the side from some difficult situations. Throughout the season he has saved many goals by his judgment and anticipation, frequently springing up 'from nowhere' to save what looked like certain goals." Baker was later a publican in Leeds and Chapeltown, and became a director of Leeds United from July 1958 to 1961.
Appearances: FL: 28 apps 6 gls FAC: 2 apps 0 gls Total: 30 apps 6 gls
Honours: Leeds United Division Two champions 1924.

BAKER, Lawrence Henry

Half-back 5' 10" 12st 0lbs
Born: Sheffield, 18 November 1897
Died: Barnsley, January quarter 1979
Career: Darnell Old Boys. Beighton. Blackpool August 1919. Leeds United May 1923. Barnsley March 1925. Rochdale May 1929. Nelson August 1930 to 27th March 1931, when contract cancelled.
Debut v Hull City (a) 2.9.30, lost 0–2
The son of a Somerset-born Policeman, Lawrie Baker began with Blackpool in Division Two, making his debut in a 1–0 win against Bury on 2nd April 1920. After 19 appearances he joined Leeds United, following his manager Bill Norman to Elland Road. He was a West Riding Cup winner in 1923 and a finalist in 1924 but played in only 11 League matches before joining Barnsley, where he finally enjoyed lengthy spells of first team football (78 League matches). A season with Rochdale (34 League matches) preceded his final season with Nelson in which he failed to hold his place and was released at the end of March.
Appearances: FL: 7 apps 0 gls Total: 7 apps 0 gls

BALDWIN, Joseph

Inside-right 5' 10" 11st 7lbs
Born: Blackburn
Career: Thought to have been an amateur on Blackburn Rover's books prior to joining NELSON as an amateur July 1929
Debut v Darlington (h) 11.9.30, lost 0–1
Reserve team forward Joe Baldwin was introduced to League action in a team showing wholesale changes for the midweek visit of Darlington to Seedhill. A spate of early season injuries had sidelined Kelly, Metcalfe and Ferguson, but it was a surprise when another new goalkeeper, Shevlin, who had been signed on the morning of the match, became the fourth new custodian of the season – after just four matches! In delightful weather and before a "gate" of 4.002 spectators, Darlington proved to be the much cleverer side and might have won by a higher margin. Baldwin, clearly out of his class, was seldom seen throughout the game, and returned to reserve team football.
Appearances: FL: 1 app 0 gls Total: 1 app 0 gls

BATE, Arthur

Centre-forward or Outside-right 5' 8½" 12st 0lbs
Born: Little Hulton, 14 October 1908
Died: Lancaster, February 1993
Career: Walkden P.M. Bury (trial). Little Hulton United. Winsford United (trial) August 1929. Chorley October 1929. Nelson July 1930 to May 1931. Chorley January 1932. Bacup Borough September 1932. Fleetwood September 1934. Bacup Borough November 1934.
Debut v Rochdale (a) 30.8.30, lost 4–5 (scored a hat-trick)
It would not be difficult to imagine Arthur Bate's mixed feelings after he had scored a hat-trick on his debut at Rochdale but still finished on the

losing side. Inside two minutes Bate had neatly lobbed the ball over the head of Rochdale's advancing goalkeeper, Jack Prince. Rochdale quickly fought back and were in front on twelve minutes before Tom Carmedy found the net for Nelson with a low drive after 16 minutes. The glut of goals continued, Bate flicking the ball into the net from close range after 24 minutes. In a game rich with hectic goalmouth melees, Rochdale led 4–3 on the hour, but Bate was again on hand to score after 70 minutes. Despite heroics from Nelson's goalkeeper Shevlin, Rochdale went in front for the last time through Tippett with five minutes remaining. One week later, Arthur Bate scored twice in a 3–1 victory against Darlington, but the goals dried up and he was out of the side for two months in mid season, returning for a spell at outside-right before reverting to centre-forward for his, and the club's, final four matches in the Football League.

Appearances: FL: 24 apps 6 gls FAC: 2 apps 0 gls
Total: 26 apps 6 gls

BEDFORD, Lewis 'Lew'

Outside-left　　5'6"　　10st 7lbs
Born: Aston, July quarter 1899
Died: Birmingham, 29 June 1966
Career: Icknield Street School. West Bromwich Albion amateur November 1920, professional March 1921. Walsall June 1922. Sheffield Wednesday August 1925, fee £575. Walsall September 1926, fee £200. Nelson March 1927. Walsall February 1928. Luton Town April 1928. Walsall December 1929. Bloxwich Strollers 1931. Walsall Wood to June 1940.
Debut v Accrington Stanley (a) 12.3.27, won 7–0, (scored two.)

Lew Bedford obviously had a strong affection for Walsall FC and the club for him when one considers the number of occasions that he found employment with the Saddlers. In four separate spells the sprightly little wingman amassed 147 League and Cup appearances and scored 13 goals. He began with West Bromwich Albion but made only three first team appearances before embarking on his travels, a highlight along the way being his 11 appearances and two goals for Sheffield Wednesday in their Division Two championship side of 1925-26. He made an immediate impact on arrival at Seedhill, scoring twice in the season's best victory, 7–0 against Accrington Stanley. In the following season, the sale of Jimmy Hampson to Blackpool after nine matches saw the team's fortunes in steep decline, and Bedford returned to Walsall before the end of the season. In a Luton Town side that also featured two other ex-Nelson players, Harry Abbott and John Black, Bedford scored on his debut and netted 13 goals in 40 League and Cup matches in 1928-29. A final spell with his first love, Walsall, preceded his move into non-League circles, initially with Bloxwich Strollers. Outside of football, Bedford worked as a foreman in a Midlands based mineral water company.
Appearances: FL: 32 apps 7 gls Total: 32 apps 7 gls

BENNETT, William

Inside-right
5' 10½"　　12st 0lbs
Born: Leyland, 1896
Career: Leyland Motors. Sheffield United February 1921. Leyland Motors January 1922. Chorley March 1922. NELSON June 1922. Leyland Motors March 1923. Lytham September 1924. Leyland Motors by December 1925.
Debut v Rochdale (h) 25.11.22, lost 1–2

A keen overnight frost made playing conditions difficult on a hard and slippery surface, but Rochdale proved to be the more capable side in the top of the table clash at Seedhill that marked the debut of William Bennett, introduced in place of the injured Arthur Wolstenholme. Nelson's forwards seldom moved in unison, despite a re-arrangement in the second half that featured Eddlestone at outside-right, Black inside, and Bennett at centre-forward. Said to have shown "little initiative", Bennett was not the only forward to disappoint, Parkes, the big Rochdale centre-half proving a massive stumbling block throughout.
Appearances: FL: 1 app 0 gls Total: 1 app 0 gls

19

BENNIE, John

Centre-forward
Born: Polmont, Stirlingshire, 30 November 1896
Career: Slammanan. Falkirk 1919-20. Bo'ness May 1921. NELSON amateur October, professional December 1921. Bo'ness May 1922.
Debut v Chesterfield (a) 22.10.21, won 2–1

John Bennie began with Falkirk but played in only 14 matches in two seasons. Dropping down a division, he did much better with Bo'ness. The West Lothian side moved up from the Central League to commence in Division Two of the Scottish League from season 1921-22, and Bennie's displays came to the attention of Nelson's scouts, leading to his recruitment, initially on amateur forms, in October of Nelson's first season in the Football League. The Scottish attack leader largely failed to realise expectations, although his preference for taking the shortest route to goal led to a respectable scoring rate. In the close season he returned homewards to Newton Park, resuming his career with Bo'ness.

Appearances: FL: 12 apps 6 gls FAC: 2 apps 0 gls
Total: 14 apps 6 gls

BIRDS, Joseph

Goalkeeper
5' 9" 11st 9lbs
Born: Youlgreave, Derbyshire, 29 October 1887
Died: Stockport, 28 April 1966
Career: Manchester Schoolboys. Hazel Grove. Macclesfield Town. Stockport County amateur September 1910, professional August 1911. Wartime guest player with Manchester City. Stockport County 1919. Macclesfield Town. Nelson June 1922 to cs 1924.
Debut v Bradford Park Avenue (a) 26.8.22, lost 2–6

Joe Birds began in Division Two with Stockport County, making his debut at Huddersfield Town in a 4–1 defeat on 14th January 1911. At either side of World War One he made 38 League and Cup appearances. Recruited by Nelson for their second season as a Football League club, he missed only two matches throughout the successful campaign, conceding only 36 goals in the same number of matches as Nelson won the championship of the Third Division North. Described as a cool and clever goalkeeper, he was certainly lacking in height for his position, but he was extremely agile and a good shot-stopper. He was eventually replaced by Harry Abbott, the former Portsmouth goalkeeper, who held his position in the League side throughout the following relegation season.

Appearances: 40 apps 0 gls FAC: 2 apps 0 gls
Total: 42 apps 0 gls
Honours: NELSON, Third Division North champions 1923.

BLACK, John Ross

Utility
5' 7 ½" 10st 8lbs
Born: Dunipace, Stirlingshire, 26 May 1900
Died: Scunthorpe, December 1993
Career: Gordon Highlanders. Denny Hibernian. Sunderland amateur April, professional August 1921. NELSON August 1922. Accrington Stanley February 1924. Chesterfield June 1924, fee £25. Luton Town June 1926. Bristol Rovers October 1930 to 1932.
Debut v Southport (h) 23.9.22, won 2–0

Red-haired John Black was a player of considerable value if only for his versatility. During Nelson's championship winning side of 1922-23 he played in four forward positions and also as a half-back and full-back. The young Scotsman won junior international honours and went on to appear in all four divisions of the Football League. In his second season with Chesterfield, a broken leg sidelined him for most of the season but he made a complete recovery and later made nearly a century of appearances for Luton Town. His elder brother was Adam Black, the well known, long-serving (1920-35) full-back of Leicester City.

Appearances: FL: 29 apps 5 gls FAC: 2 apps 0 gls
Total: 31 apps 5 gls
Honours: Scotland Junior International. NELSON: Third Division North champions 1923.

BOSSONS, William Horace

Goalkeeper
Born: Lowton, Newcastle-under-Lyme, April 1901
Died: Lowton, Newcastle-under-Lyme, January quarter 1970
Career: Stockport County March 1925. Macclesfield Town November 1925. NELSON amateur September 1927 to February 1928. Whitchurch 1928-29. Winsford United July 1929. Oswestry Town October 1930.

Debut v Chesterfield (h) 8.10.27, drawn 3–3

Bossons' first appearance was with Nelson Reserves against Darwen in a Lancashire Combination fixture at Seedhill on 27th September 1927. Initially on trial from Macclesfield, his Seedhill debut was a relatively quiet one in a 3–2 victory. Nelson used four goalkeepers in Football League matches during the course of the 1927-28 season, when Nelson sought re-election for the first time, conceding 136 goals in 42 League engagements. Bossons' four first team matches resulted in one win, one draw and two defeats, with nine goals scored and fourteen conceded.

Appearances: FL: 4 apps 0 gls Total: 4 apps 0 gls

BOTTO, Lewis Anthony

Goalkeeper
5' 8"   11st 6lbs
Born: Jarrow, 12 July 1898
Died: Jarrow, 4 June 1953
Career: Jarrow Rangers. Hebburn Colliery amateur July 1923. Durham City amateur August, professional October 1923. Shildon Athletic loan August 1925. Durham City July 1926. Wolverhampton Wanderers August 1927. Norwich City October 1928. NELSON September 1929. Jarrow November 1929.
Debut v Crewe Alexandra (a) 7.10.29, lost 0–4

A confident and workmanlike goalkeeper, if on the short side for his position, Lewis Botto made 82 league appearances for Durham City in two separate spells, but played in little first team football thereafter. In 16 matches for the Wolves he was beaten 26 times, and although he was unbeaten on his Norwich City debut he played only once more before joining Nelson. Incidentally, his Norwich City debut was made under the pseudonym of G.O. Alie, and he first appeared in the local press as L. Blotto! He was one of four different goalkeepers fielded by Nelson in the first four matches of season 1929-30 (which must constitute some sort of a record!). His debut, in the season's third match, proved to be his last in League football, as the arrival of Peter Shevlin from South Shields finally solved the problems in the last line of Nelson's defence.

Appearances: FL: 1 app 0 gls Total: 1 app 0 gls

BOTTRILL, Allan

Outside-left
Born: Eston, Yorkshire, January quarter 1905
Died: Eston, Yorkshire, 29 November 1929
Career: Whitby Town. Middlesbrough amateur August, professional October 1921. NELSON January 1925. York City October 1926. South Bank East End September 1927.
Debut v Durham City (a) 29.4.25, lost 1–3

The younger brother of Nelson's Billy Bottrill, and the fourth of seven children, Allan joined Middlesbrough at the same time as his brother, but failed to graduate beyond reserve team football. He was similarly unsuccessful when he rejoined his elder brother at Seedhill. After spending his time in Nelson's Lancashire Combination side, he was handed a Football League debut in the season's final fixture. It was the only occasion that the brothers had appeared together in a League match, but Durham City spoilt their day by winning 3–1. Outside of football, Allan worked as a plater's helper in a shipyard. Tragically, he was only 24 years old when he died from acute pneumonia.

Appearances: FL: 1 app 0 gls Total: 1 app 0 gls

BOTTRILL, Walter Gibson 'Billy'

Inside-right
5' 10"   11st 7lbs
Born: Eston, Yorkshire, 8 January 1903
Died: Eston, Yorkshire, 29 September 1976
Career: South Bank. Middlesbrough amateur May, professional October 1921. NELSON June 1924, fee £250. Rotherham United July 1928. York City August 1929. Wolverhampton Wanderers May 1930. Huddersfield Town May 1933. Chesterfield October 1934.
Debut v Southport (a) 30.8.24, lost 0–1

Once described as: "A clever and adaptable schemer with a powerful shot, but at times prone to over-elaborate when in sight of goal". Billy Bottrill began as an outside-right with Middlesbrough, making his debut in Division One against local rivals Newcastle United on Boxing Day 1922. After 18 League and Cup matches he was transferred to Nelson, and for the next four seasons he was the most conspicuous member of the team's attack. He was immediately switched to inside-right at Seedhill and successfully partnered Syd Hoad until he sustained a serious injury at Grimsby Town on 14th March and missed eleven matches. He recovered in time to play in the season's last two matches, and in the following term he scored 16 goals in 38 League games. He passed the milestone of 100 League appearances for Nelson in season 1927-28, alternating between inside and outside-right during the campaign. On leaving Seedhill, he enjoyed success with both Rotherham United (30 matches, 11 goals) and York City (39 matches, 18 goals). A move to the Wolves in May 1930 brought him a Division Two championship medal in 1932 and an overall contribution of 101 League appearances and 42 goals. He appeared infrequently with Huddersfield Town and Chesterfield, but ended his career with an outstanding career aggregate of 336 League matches and 112 goals.

Appearances: FL: 121 apps 35 gls FAC: 6 apps 0 gls
Total: 127 apps 35 gls
Honours: Wolverhampton Wanderers, Division Two champions 1932

BRAIDWOOD, Ernest

Centre-half
6' 0"   12st 0lbs
Born: Heywood, 14 April 1895
Died: Heywood, 16 July 1968
Career: York Street Congregational (Heywood). Chesterfield Municipal February 1920. Oldham Athletic amateur June, professional August 1920. NELSON May 1922. Rochdale March 1926. Great Harwood February 1930. New Mills September 1930.
Debut v Bradford Park Avenue (a) 26.8.22, lost 2–6

Footballers standing six feet tall were very much a minority in the 1920s, and during his Oldham Athletic days, the popular cartoonist 'ASM' loved to depict the centre-half in skyscraper proportions. Nine First Division outings and one goal, the winner against Derby County, was an encouraging start with the Latics, but a change of manager saw him selected only once for first team duty in 1921-22. In the close season he joined forces with former team-mate David Wilson, player-manager of Nelson. Ideally built for a centre-half, he rarely had an off day and enjoyed a most successful spell at Seedhill, which included the championship success of 1923, and the runners-up spot two years later. In both of the successful campaigns he recorded maximum appearances. Braidwood subsequently came close to winning a second Third Division North championship medal with Rochdale, who finished as runners-up to Stoke in season 1926-27. A bricklayer by trade, and cousin of James Pearson (q.v.), Ernie was a member of the Central League team that played the North Eastern League in season 1920-21.

Appearances: FL: 128 apps 10 gls FAC: 7 apps 1 gl
Total: 135 apps 11 gls
Honours: NELSON, Third Division North champions 1923.

BROADHEAD, James Edward

Left-half
5' 10½"   11st 7lbs
Born: Rotherham, 25 August 1894
Died: Whiston, near Prescot, 4 May 1955.
Career: Kimberworth Old Boys 1912. Rotherham County 1913. Norwich City May 1919. South Shields May 1920. Scunthorpe & Lindsay United January 1921. NELSON May 1922. Barnoldswick Town July 1926. NELSON, reserve team player-coach May 1927. Horwich RMI 1928. Morecambe July 1930. NELSON trainer. Southampton coaching staff August 1935.
Debut v Bradford Park Avenue (a) 26.8.22, lost 2–6

Ted Broadhead joined Nelson from Scunthorpe & Lindsay United, signing off his career with the "Nuts" by scoring in the season's final Midland League fixture, a 1–1 draw against Harrogate. He had commenced with Rotherham County before the Great War and joined Norwich City for their resumption in the Southern League in 1919-20. Operating at either inside-right or centre-forward, he netted eight goals in 31 matches. Failing to make a first team appearance during his sojourn with South Shields, he was transferred in mid season to Scunthorpe & Lindsay United, joining Nelson for their second season in the Football League. The tall, fair-haired wing-half was a tireless worker who made particularly good use of the ground pass. He served Nelson wholeheartedly as a player, coach and trainer in a lengthy association, the highlights being his involvement in two championship-winning sides. He missed only two matches in the Third Division North championship side of 1922-23, and three years later, he captained the reserve team to the championship of the Lancashire Combination, after making a successful recovery from a knee injury. Ted Broadhead settled at Whiston, near Prescot and worked for Littlewoods of Liverpool. The two medals that he won during his Nelson career were recently sold by Sportingold Ltd, the Saunderton-based auctioneers of football and sport memorabilia.

Appearances: FL: 67 apps 1 gl FAC: 2 apps 0 gls Total: 69 apps 1 gl
Honours: NELSON, Third Division North champions 1923.

BROADHURST, Fred

Right-back   5' 8½"   11st 6lbs
Born: Hindley, 30 November 1888
Died: Aspull, 9 May 1953
Career: Hindley Central. Preston North End amateur April, professional May 1910. Hindley Central (loan) March 1913. Stalybridge Celtic June 1922. Stockport County May 1923. Barrow June 1924. NELSON July 1925. Chorley July 1927.
Debut v Crewe Alexandra (h) 29.8.25, won 2-1
Despite being well into the veteran stage when signed, Fred Broadhurst gave extremely good value during two seasons at Seedhill, being particularly impressive during a run of 37 consecutive appearances in his first season. Resolute first-time tackling and well placed clearances being a feature of his game. He began with Preston North End and in a lengthy stay at Deepdale completed 115 League and Cup appearances and was awarded £400 in lieu of a benefit in season 1919-20. He subsequently made 36 appearances for Stalybridge Celtic in their second season in the Football League, but played in only four matches for Stockport County before joining Barrow. In an excellent season at Holker Street the veteran defender recorded 47 League and Cup appearances before winding-up his senior career with Nelson. His overall career figures amounted to 246 League matches and three goals.

Appearances: FL: 61 apps 0 gls FAC: 3 apps 0 gls Total: 64 apps 0 gls

BROOKS, John 'Jack'

Right-back   5' 10"   12st 10lbs
Born: Stockton-on-Tees, 13 March 1904
Died: Stockton-on-Tees, 30 March 1973
Career: Stillington St John's. Fulham May 1924. Darlington June 1926. NELSON March 1929. York City August 1929 to February 1932. Bacup Borough September 1934. ICI – General Chemicals of Durham - reinstated amateur October 1936.
Debut v Wigan Borough (h) 16.3.29, won 2-1
Burly full-back Jack Brooks made his League debut with Fulham in a 1-0 away win at Port Vale on 8th September 1924. He made only six League appearances in two years at Craven Cottage, and six in his first season with Darlington, who were relegated from Division Two. He established himself at right-back in the following season, however, appearing in 36 League and three FA Cup matches. He joined Nelson in March of the following season, but in the summer was released and joined York City. The Minstermen had an eventful first season in the Football League, finishing in sixth place in the Northern Section and enjoying a memorable run in the FA Cup, only losing after a replay against First Division opponents Newcastle United, after they had held them to a 1–1 draw at St James' Park in round three. After 93 League and Cup matches he left Bootham Crescent, ending his playing days in the Lancashire Combination with Bacup Borough. During his spell with Fulham, Brooks was awarded a gold medal after giving blood at the scene of a crash when travelling to White Hart Lane for a reserve team match against Tottenham Hotspur. His prompt and selfless action saved the life of Fulham's trainer, Elijah Morse, whose severe injuries resulted in the loss of an arm.

Appearances: FL: 6 apps 0 gls Total: 6 apps 0 gls

BROWN, Alfred

Left-half 5' 8"   11st 7lbs
Born: Sheffield, 27 December 1898
Career: Sheffield Schoolboys. Carbrook Reform. Sheffield United April 1918. Rotherham Town July 1919. Blackpool May 1921. Barnsley May 1923. Swindon Town August 1926. NELSON (trial) September-October 1927. Barnsley (trial). Hurst. Manchester Central November 1929. Stalybridge Celtic June 1932
Debut v Durham City (h) 24 September 1927, won 2-1

Said to have played vigorously on his debut, but without any constructiveness in his work, the hard-to-please local correspondent also observed that wing half-back Alf Brown, on trial from Swindon Town, "Frequently booted the ball like a full-back." The 2-1 victory against Durham City also marked the debuts of goalkeeper Sam Warhurst, a local lad, and left-back David McClure, who was unfortunately debited with an own-goal on his first appearance. Alf Brown played once more for Nelson, in a 3-1 defeat at Barrow, before being released on 17th October.
Appearances: FL: 2 apps 0 gls Total: 2 apps 0 gls

BROWN, John

Outside-right
5' 7"   11st 10lbs
Born: Glasgow
Career: Broxburn. Armadale. Shawfield. East Stirlingshire August 1921. St Johnstone (trial). Brechin City. Morton 1925-26. Burnley (trial) January 1927. NELSON (trial) February to March 1927. Manchester Central.
Debut v Bradford Park Avenue (h) 12.2.27, won 1-0

Nelson had to reconstruct their forward line for the visit of Bradford Park Avenue in February 1927. Due to the absence of Sharp, who was down with 'flu, Stevenson went to inside-left, Bottrill to inside-right, and John Brown made his Football League debut at outside-right. Overnight frost had made the pitch very hard and difficult for the players, but the best home "gate" of the season (12,415) witnessed an exciting game, won by a single goal scored after just two minutes play. Baker's weak shot struck Bradford's captain, Fell, goalkeeper Clough slipped in the treacherous goalmouth and the diverted ball found the back of the net. Newcomer Brown was said to be very speedy and persistent, but his centring was poor and it was thought that he might have been more effective in different conditions. In Scottish football, Brown completed 21 first team appearances for Morton and scored seven goals. Following Morton's relegation from Division One in 1927, he spent a month on trial with both Burnley and Nelson, but failed to secure a permanent engagement.
Appearances: FL: 2 apps 0 gls Total: 2 apps 0 gls

BRUCE, Robert Fotheringham

Goalkeeper   5' 10"
Born: Bridge of Allan, Stirlingshire, 1895
Career: Cowie Wanderers. Kirkintilloch Rob Roy. Raith Rovers 1916. Partick Thistle February 1917 to April 1918. Alloa Athletic May 1919. Kirkintilloch Rob Roy 1920. NELSON October 1921, Plean cs 1922. Stenhousemuir. Broxburn United.
Debut v Chesterfield (a) 22.10.21, won 2-1

Robert Bruce's best spell in Scottish senior football came with Partick Thistle, for whom he made his debut in a 1-0 home win against Clyde on 9th April 1916. Living at that time in Cowie, his contract was for £1 per week and 4 shillings and six pence travelling expenses. In the following season he played in 16 First Division matches and in the Glasgow Charity Cup Final at Hampden Park, won 2-0 by Celtic. In post war football he was a Scottish Junior Cup winner with Kirkintilloch Rob Roy before joining Nelson in October 1921. His ten first team appearances were made consecutively and commenced in promising fashion with a 'double' against Chesterfield, 2-1 at Saltergate and 2-0 at Seedhill one week later. He lost his place after a disappointing 5-3 home defeat by Durham City on Boxing Day and did not reappear in the League side, returning to Scotland in the close season.
Appearances: FL: 7 apps 0 gls FAC: 3 apps 0 gls Total: 10 apps 0 gls

BUCHANAN, James

Inside-right
5' 9"   11st 7lbs
Born: Kirkliston, near Winchburgh, West Lothian, 10 October 1898
Career: Bellstone Birds. Winchburgh Violet. Broxburn United. Aberdeen (trial) November 1920. Hibernian December 1920. Bournemouth & Boscombe Athletic May 1924. Raith Rovers (loan) June 1925. East Stirlingshire August 1928. NELSON September 1928. Ashton National (trial) August 1930. Clitheroe August 1930. Accrington Stanley October-December 1930. Bray Unknowns. Shamrock Rovers August 1932. Bangor (Northern Ireland) August 1935 to May 1936.
Debut v Barrow (h) 13.10.28, lost 3-4

Jim Buchanan began as a centre-forward with Broxburn United, but it was soon found that he was more suited to the outside-right position. An extremely clever player with a good burst of speed, he was signed by Hibernian as understudy to H.G. Ritchie, the Scottish international. He spent a little over three seasons with the Hibs and won a string of minor honours that included the East of Scotland Shield, the Wilson Cup, the Dunedin Cup and the Rosebery Charity Cup. He first crossed the border in May 1924 when he joined Bournemouth on a free transfer. At the time he received a number of offers, the lowest being from Bournemouth, who were not in a position to offer such good terms as other clubs. His wife, however, made the decision for him, considering that Bournemouth would be a nice place to live! After 75 League and Cup appearances he returned briefly to Scotland to sign for East Stirlingshire before joining Nelson following a successful trial. Considering that Nelson fielded an almost totally re-constructed team from that that finished at the foot of the table in 1927-28, an advance to 15th position was considered a satisfactory performance. In 32 consecutive appearances at inside-right Buchanan supplied much of the ammunition for Bernard Radford's successful goal-scoring return of 24 in 35 League matches. Retained for a further season, Buchanan scored nine goals in 34 League matches but could do little to halt a slump that saw the side win only once in the season's final twelve fixtures.
Appearances: FL: 66 apps 15 gls FAC: 1 app 0 gls
Total: 67 apps 15 gls

BUTTERWORTH, Herbert

Left-half 5' 10"   11st 4lbs
Born: Higham, Lancashire, July quarter 1902
Career: Higham FC. Wolverhampton Wanderers November 1920. NELSON amateur August 1923, professional January 1925. Colne Town August 1926. Great Harwood December 1926. Wellington Town August 1927. Colne Town. C.P.R. Calgury (Canada) May 1929. Trent Motors (Derby) amateur October 1936.
Debut v Tranmere Rovers (h) 7.2.25, won 4-1

A weaver by profession, Herbert Butterworth began in Padiham & District League football and won the championship with the Higham club in 1923. Shortly after signing professional forms with Nelson, he made his League debut and held his place for seven consecutive matches, the first five of which yielded maximum points. During the successful run he was reported to have played a "blinder" against New Brighton and "was the best half-back on the field". Despite the promising start, he was almost exclusively a reserve team player in 1925-26 when the team won the Lancashire Combination championship and were finalists in the Combination Cup. On 8th March 1929 he sailed to Halifax, Canada, on the White Star liner Regina.
Appearances: FL: 9 apps 0 gls Total: 9 apps 0 gls

CAINE, James

Centre-half
5' 9½"   11st 6lbs
Born: Brierfield, 24 June 1908
Died: Walton Lane, Nelson, 9 May 1971
Career: Brierfield R.C. Brierfield Schoolboys. Burnley December 1927. NELSON September 1929. Brierfield R.C. Bury August 1931. Barnoldswick Town. William Fell & Co. (Nelson) amateur January 1935.
Debut v Doncaster

25

Rovers (a) 1.3.30, lost 0–3

Despite association with three Football League clubs, Jimmy Caine's only senior involvement was with Nelson. Although playing regularly in the reserve team, and being considered a player in the making, the powerfully built defender played in just two Football League matches in 1929-30, and in three in the following season. On leaving the professional ranks, he assisted William Fell & Co. Ltd., Pendle Street Mills, Nelson, plain and fancy weavers and yarn dyers and bleachers. All six of Jimmy Caine's sons played football. Brian, the only one to play professionally, was an ideally built goalkeeper who assisted a number of League clubs in the 1950s and early sixties, most notably with Barrow, for whom he appeared in 119 League and Cup matches in three seasons at Holker Street.

Appearances: FL: 5 apps 0 gls Total: 5 apps 0 gls

CAMERON, Edward S.

Outside-left 5' 7½" 11st 7lbs
Born: Glasgow
Career: Clydebank cs 1919. Birmingham July 1921. Walsall May 1922. NELSON March 1924, fee £100. Stafford Rangers May 1926. Exeter City June 1928. Stafford Rangers April 1929. NELSON (trial) cs 1929. Cradley Heath Alliance February 1932. Hednesford Town September 1932. Stafford Rangers July 1934.
Debut v Barnsley (a) 15.3.24, drawn 0–0

'The Lancashire Daily Post' had a special word of praise for Eddie Cameron, after he had created a good impression in his first two outings in Nelson's colours: "He is sturdily built, very speedy, and not without craft, and is certainly the best occupant of the outside-left position in the Nelson team this season." Sadly, his arrival came too late to prevent his new team from being relegated, after a single season in Division Two. Back in the more familiar surroundings of the Third Division North, he continued to impress, missing only four League matches in 1924-25, when the team came very close to winning back their Second Division status. In the event, they won only one of their final five fixtures and finished as runners-up to Darlington.

Appearances: FL: 46 apps 10 gls FAC: 1 app 0 gls
Total: 47 apps 10 gls

CARMEDY, Thomas Owen 'Tom'

Centre-forward 5' 9½" 11st 7lbs
Born: Gainford, County Durham, 23 June 1904
Died: Weybridge, January 1985
Career: Gainford FC. Darlington amateur March 1927. Cockfield amateur November 1927. Bishop Auckland 1927-28. NELSON amateur December 1928, professional January 1929. Barrow June 1931. Boston Town October 1932. Northwood United November 1933.
Debut v Southport (h) 19.1.29, drawn 1–1 (scored)

Tom Carmedy played in one Football League match for Darlington, making his debut as an amateur at Bradford City on 31st August 1927 in a 1–0 victory. Some sixteen months later he returned to League football with Nelson, quickly winning a professional contract after just a month on amateur forms. During his two and a half seasons at Seedhill he proved a willing and adaptable forward, occupying at various times every position across the front rank, although he was most effective at centre-forward. His two hat-tricks – scored a year apart – were netted from the vanguard of the attack. In March 1931 his extreme versatility was put to the test when, in an emergency, he donned the goalkeeper's jersey for the reserves in their Combination fixture against Lancaster Town at Seedhill. A heavy fall of snow during the morning of the match had left the pitch under a six-inch layer of snow. The ball stopped where it dropped and players were unable to keep their feet. Although Nelson lost 4–1, a report of the match left no doubt that Nelson owed much to their makeshift goalkeeper, whose performance under the conditions was nothing short of remarkable. In his more accustomed role, Carmedy's last Nelson goal was scored at Barrow in April 1931, and two months later he moved to Holker Street, following Nelson's failure to gain re-election. Tom Carmedy's earliest days were spent in a Roman Catholic home in County Durham. After football he worked in a tailoring shop.

Appearances: FL: 66 apps 20 gls FAC: 1 app 0 gls Total: 67 apps 20 gls

CAULFIELD, William 'Billy'

Inside or Outside-right   5' 6"   11st 5lbs
Born: Haydock, 20 March 1892
Died: Haydock, January quarter 1972
Career: Ormskirk. Southport Central cs 1913. Blackburn Rovers February 1915. Crewe Alexandra amateur cs 1920, professional May 1921. NELSON July 1923. Crewe Alexandra September 1924. Chester cs 1925.
Debut v Coventry City (h) 3.11.23, won 3–0 (scored two)

Billy Caulfield had often been a thorn in the flesh of Nelson when opposing them in earlier days with both Southport and Crewe Alexandra. In addition to possessing excellent ball control, he had a deadly shot, and was one of the best penalty kick takers in the country. The former collier was unfortunate to sustain a groin strain in pre-season practice at Seedhill and was sidelined throughout the first three months of the season. Despite netting twice on his debut, he failed to maintain his excellent start as the team squandered their hard won promotion by finishing in 21st place in their solitary season in Division Two.

Appearances: FL: 18 apps 5 gls Total: 18 apps 5 gls

CHADWICK, Edgar

Inside-left   5' 8½"   11st 0lbs
Born: Blackburn, March 1891
Died: Nelson, January quarter 1963
Career: Army football. Blackburn Rovers "A" November 1916. NELSON January 1920. Accrington Stanley March 1921. Seedhill FC. Great Harwood August 1921. Bacup Borough. NELSON June 1923. Lancaster Town May 1926. Clitheroe May 1927. Morecambe. Bacup Borough August 1929. NELSON August 1932, appointed trainer August 1935. Nelson Town October 1936. NELSON Committee June 1946.
Debut v Hull City (h) 15.9.23, drawn 1–1

A weaver in a local cotton mill, Edgar Chadwick began with Nelson during their run of two seasons in the Central League, having had considerable experience in Army football and with Blackburn Rovers "A" Team. He returned to Seedhill in June 1923 and made his initial bow before a League crowd at outside-right in Division Two against Hull City. As the local correspondent pointed out "A few short months ago he was playing for Bacup Borough in the West Lancashire League". Nevertheless, he rounded off his first season by scoring Nelson's last goal in Division Two in a 3–1 home win against Leeds United on the final day of the season. With his favoured right wing spot dominated by England amateur international Syd Hoad, in the following season he was tried at inside-left in place of O'Beirne. Adapting well to his new role, Chadwick netted 10 goals in just 20 League matches, a valuable contribution in the team's excellent performance in finishing runners-up to Darlington. In his final season of League action (1925-26) his eight goals from just 13 League matches included a hat-trick in a 5–2

win against Hartlepools United at Seedhill in October 1925. Edgar Chadwick returned to assist Nelson in 1932, serving as player, trainer, and finally committee member in post-war years.
Appearances: FL: 36 apps 19 gls FAC: 1 app 0 gls Total: 37 apps 19 gls

CHADWICK, Walter Russell

Right-back   5' 10"   12st 0lbs
Born: Haslingden, October quarter 1903
Died: Nelson, 20 October 1966
Career: St Saviour's S.S. Burnley amateur 1923-24. Barnoldswick Town June 1924. Burnley August 1924. NELSON August 1925. Darwen June 1927.
Debut v Grimsby Town (a) 17.4.26, lost 0–3
James Pearson and Walter Chadwick were the regular full-back pairing in Nelson's Reserve side in season 1925-26. Despite using no fewer than 41 players during the season the second string showed remarkable consistency by winning 27 games against 12 in the previous season. Effectively skippered by J.E. Broadhead, the team won the championship of the Lancashire Combination for the first time. Chadwick did less well with Darwen in 1927-28 who secured only 26 points from 38 games and had to seek re-election.
Appearances: FL: 2 apps 0 gls Total: 2 apps 0 gls

CHAPMAN, Ralph

Outside-right   5' 7"   10st 7lbs
Born: Salford, 26 January 1906
Died: Peterborough, March 1999
Career: Bolton junior football. NELSON amateur November 1929 to cs 1931.
Debut v Lincoln City (a) 15.3.30, lost 1–4
As an amateur player, Ralph Chapman would not have qualified for a bonus had he finished on the winning side. That said, the matter was purely academic as his ten senior appearances yielded but a single point, one draw and nine defeats being his unhappy involvement at senior level. As a recruit from Bolton junior football, he could not have been expected to reverse the tide of defeats that engulfed the team in their final two seasons in the Football League. As the 'Nelson Leader' dolefully reported: "We have not yet reached the time when 'Ichabod' will have to be inscribed over the portals of the Nelson club, but without some drastic improvement it will surely come."
Appearances: FL: 10 apps 0 gls Total: 10 apps 0 gl

CLAYTON, Harry

Right-half   5' 11"   12st 0lbs
Born: Nelson, October quarter 1904
Career: Hebden Bridge. Chorley circa 1922. Stoke "A". Chorley April 1924. NELSON May 1924. Morecambe July 1926. Manchester Central June 1929. Central FC (Belle Vue) by early 1931. Bacup Borough. James Clark Ltd (Nelson) amateur December 1934. Lustrafil Ltd (Nelson) amateur January 1936.
Debut v Southport (a) 23.1.26, lost 1–2
Aside from four first team outings in season 1925-26, local utility defender Harry Clayton played most of his football in the Lancashire Combination, and was a member of Nelson's Reserve side who lifted the trophy in his second season at Seedhill. His first season with Morecambe was an unqualified success, appearing in 45 matches during the campaign, he assisted his new team to win the Lancashire Junior Cup, The Combination Cup for the first time, and they also finished third in the league.
Appearances: FL: 4 apps 0 gls Total: 4 apps 0 gls

CLEGG, Harry

Goalkeeper   5' 10"   11st 4lbs
Born: Burnley, circa 1895
Career: Burnley Tramways. NELSON 1920, registered for FL matches September 1921 to March 1924. Burnley Tramways amateur March 1928.
Debut v Accrington Stanley (h) 15.10.21, lost 0–1
Despite being short of experience, Harry Clegg was said to have made "a few good saves" on his debut in League football, when he was a late replacement for regular 'keeper Harry Heyes. His form and confidence improved rapidly thereafter and he made a further four League appearances in 1921-22. He was subsequently confined to reserve team football as the first team jersey was dominated in turn by experienced custodians Joe Birds and Harry Abbott. The former Burnley Tramways goalkeeper nevertheless was the championship team's last line of defence in their ground-breaking summer tour to Spain in 1924.
Appearances: FL: 5 apps 0 gls Total: 5 apps 0 gls

COCHRANE, David Stobbie

Centre-forward   5' 9"   11st 2lbs
Born: Dunblane, 30 January 1910
Career: Dunblane Rovers. Denny Hibernian. NELSON November 1927. Bo'ness January 1928. Armadale March 1928.
Debut v Bradford City (a) 12.11.27, lost 1–9 (scored)
David Cochrane's excellent goal-scoring record with Denny included 16 in the early months of

season 1927-28, his total including four on the Saturday prior to his arrival at Seedhill. He was recommended to Nelson by their former player, Mick McCulloch, but sadly failed to settle and returned to Scotland after the briefest of stays. His sojourn was not uneventful, nine goals being conceded on his scoring debut at Bradford City. Seven days later he netted again in a 3–2 home win against Halifax Town. Granted a free transfer he joined Bo'ness, but within a matter of weeks he was on the move again, joining Armadale along with Bo'ness half-back James Kelly.
Appearances: FL: 2 apps 2 gls FAC: 1 app 0 gls
Total: 3 apps 2 gls

COLLINS, Legh Richman

Half-back 5' 8½" 11st 0lbs
Born: Liverpool, 5 March 1901
Died: Birkenhead, October quarter 1975
Career: Liverpool Schoolboys. Grassendale St Mary's. Wigan Borough amateur November 1921, professional February 1922. NELSON May 1923. New Brighton July 1924. Crewe Alexandra October 1925. Stalybridge Celtic.
Debut v Hull City (a) 8.9.23, lost 1–2
Once described as "A neat footballer and a keen tackler," Collins began with Wigan Borough, appearing in their first season as a Football League club. At Seedhill, he initially contested the left-half position with Broadhead, in Nelson's only season of Second Division football. Moving on to New Brighton, he assisted the Rakers to their best ever placing, third in the Northern Section of Division Three. In May 1925 he was chosen to represent the Midland Combination versus the Champions (Chesterfield). He did not appear at senior level with Crewe Alexandra, his final League club.
Appearances: FL: 13 apps 0 gls FAC: 2 apps 0 gls
Total: 15 apps 0 gls

COUNSELL, Henry James 'Harry'

Right-back 5' 9" 10st 10lbs
Born: Preston, 10 April 1909
Died: Burnley, January 1990
Career: Great Marsden School (Nelson). Chorley. NELSON amateur from season 1929-30, registered for Football League matches March 1931. Great Harwood. Clitheroe August 1933. Lancaster Town August 1935.
Debut v Rotherham United (a) 28.3.31, lost 0–3
Harry Counsell starred in local schools football and was first associated with Nelson during season 1929-30, although he was not registered to play in Football League matches until March 1931. At this point he deputised for Gilbert Richmond in three matches. The last two coming within a day of each other on the 3rd and 4th of April, a 2–1 victory over Wigan Borough being followed by a 5–0 defeat by Chesterfield. Harry Counsell remained at Seedhill for the start of the 1931-32 season, the team recommencing in the Lancashire Combination with a home match against Horwich RMI. The club announced reduced prices of admission (six pence) and season tickets were available, the most expensive centre stand ticket costing just £1.
Appearances: FL: 3 apps 0 gls Total: 3 apps 0 gls

COWEN, James Ernest

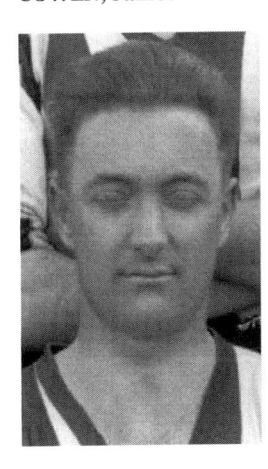

Centre-forward 5' 10" 11st 7lbs
Born: Dyon Side, Distington, 22 January 1902
Died: Peterborough, 5 July 1950
Career: Hensingham FC. Whitehaven Athletic. NELSON November 1925. Barnoldswick Town August 1926. Northampton Town May 1927. Southport August 1929. Aldershot August 1933.

Peterborough United June 1934. Westwood Works reinstated amateur July 1935. Peterborough Post Office Engineers November 1936.
Debut v Grimsby Town (h) 5.12.25, drawn 1–1 (scored)

With Joe Eddleston and the emerging Jimmy Hampson as direct competition, reserve centre-forward Jimmy Cowen was offered few opportunities, but he assisted Nelson's Lancashire Combination side to carry off the title for the first time in 1925-26. His 24 goals for the season included five against Great Harwood in a 10–1 victory in December, the side scoring 123 goals during the season, in which they narrowly failed to achieve a double by finishing as runners-up to Fleetwood for the Combination Cup. Moving to Victory Park, along with Ted Broadhead, the pair had the satisfaction of scoring both of Barnoldswick's goals in their 2–1 victory against Nelson Reserves in February 1927. Cowen played regularly in League football for the first time with Southport and scored 55 goals in 129 matches in four seasons at Haig Avenue. When his playing career ended he worked as an electrical engineer for the GPO at Peterborough. He was only 48 years old when he died, after a long illness, at Peterborough Memorial Hospital.

Appearances: FL: 3 apps 4 gls Total: 3 apps 4 gls

CRAWSHAW, Richard Leigh

Inside-left   5' 7½"   10st 10lbs
Born: Prestwich, Manchester, 21 September 1898
Died: Manchester, 23 October 1965
Career: Newton Heath School. Woodhouses FC. During WW1 assisted Stockport County, Accrington Stanley and Rochdale. Manchester City June 1919. Halifax Town July 1922. NELSON February 1923, fee £100. Stalybridge Celtic June 1924. Mossley June 1929 to May 1931.

Debut v Wigan Borough (a) 24.2.23, won 1–0 (scored)

An all-round sportsman who listed his other interests as swimming, tennis and cricket, Crawshaw served in the Royal Navy during the Great War. He commenced in Division One with Manchester City and scored on his debut against Bolton Wanderers in September 1919. The lively and bustling newcomer scored six goals in 21 League matches in his first season, but was mainly in reserve during 1920-21 when City finished as runners-up for the League Championship. He arrived at Nelson from Halifax Town, scored the winner on his debut, and played in the final 13 matches of the season, winning a Third Division North Championship medal. During Nelson's summer tour of Spain in 1923 he scored the team's first goal against Racing Club Santander and, five days later, scored twice in the famous 4–2 victory against Real Madrid. His vigorous approach and direct methods were less effective in Division Two, but he netted the season's only hat-trick in the 4–1 victory against Crystal Palace at Seedhill in October 1923. During the late stages of his career he was chosen to represent the Cheshire League versus the Welsh League in March 1928. A nephew, Richard Duckworth, assisted several League clubs during the 1920s and thirties.

Appearances: FL: 32 apps 10 gls FAC: 2 apps 0 gls Total: 34 apps 10 gls
Honours: NELSON: Third Division North champions 1923.

DARGAN, James

Inside-right   5' 9"   11st 8lbs
Born: Manchester, 28 August 1906
Died: Harlow, May 1985
Career: Northwich Victoria 1925-26. NELSON amateur January 1928. Northwich Victoria cs 1928. Clitheroe August 1930. Barnoldswick Town 1930. Morecambe November 1930. McMahon's FC (Manchester) July 1931.
Debut v Rotherham United (a) 21.1.28, lost 3–4

Nelson were leaking goals at an alarming rate in season 1927-28, the four conceded on the occasion of Dargan's debut at Rotherham made the total 25 in the last five matches, and the inability to stem the flow caused the team to finish at the foot of the table. Scoring goals was less of a problem, 76 goals in 42 matches was a reasonable return, the same total scored by Accrington Stanley saw them finish in ninth place, but they conceded only 67 goals whereas Nelson shipped a record 136. Recruited from Cheshire League football, Dargan made little impact on his debut despite narrowly missing a goal on debut when Rotherham's goalkeeper, Atter, did well to keep out his goal bound header. **Note**: *The player's surname, as*

recorded in contemporary match reports and in the archives of the Football League, is Dargon. His birth and death certificate, however, have the spelling Dargan.
Appearances: FL: 2 apps 0 gls Total: 2 apps 0 gls

DAWSON, Arthur

Outside-left   5' 8"   10st 6lbs
Born: Cliviger, 22 April 1907
Died: Shrewsbury, April 1985
Career: Portsmouth Rovers. Burnley amateur August, professional September 1928. Lancaster Town June 1929. NELSON September 1930 to December 1930 and re-signed for a second time in March 1931.
Debut v Carlisle United (a) 14.3.31, lost 1–8
A nephew of the famous Burnley goalkeeper, 'Jerry' Dawson, Arthur also joined Burnley but after 15 Central League appearances in 1928-29 he was released and joined Lancaster Town. He was not a regular first team player in the side that carried off the Combination championship in 1929-30, and he did not feature in Nelson's League side in his first spell, his ten appearances coinciding with the final matches of season 1930-31. The light-weight outside-left could do little to arrest the run of heavy defeats that finally sealed Nelson's fate, his eleven outings resulting in one win and ten defeats with a goal average of 9 for and 40 against – truly relegation form with a vengeance!
Appearances: FL: 10 apps 0 gls Total: 10 apps 0 gls

DENWOOD, Wilfred

Outside-left
Born: Heywood, 26 March 1900
Died: Heywood, 26 October 1959
Career: Bacup Borough July 1923. New Brighton February 1925. NELSON (trial) August-September 1925. Witton Albion July 1926. Heywood Street United Methodists amateur September 1927. Horwich RMI amateur September 1928. Heywood St James amateur September 1929.
Debut v Crewe Alexandra (h) 29.8.25, won 2–1
Wilf Denwood made his League debut for New Brighton against Nelson at Seedhill on 7th March 1925, and finished on the losing side, Nelson scoring five goals without reply. He spent much of his sojourn with the Rakers in the Midland Combination side, and was busy on Easter Monday 1925 when he played in two games. In the morning he scored once at Anfield in the reserves 5–0 win against Fairres in the Liverpool Challenge Cup Final. In the afternoon he was on the mark again, scoring for the reserves in the 4–0 win against Halifax Town Reserves at Sandheys Park. On arrival at Seedhill, he impressed in the two pre-season trial matches, but did less well in the League side, failing to win an extension to his two-month trial period.
Appearances: FL: 3 apps 0 gls Total: 3 apps 0 gls

DIXON, Charles Hubert

Centre-half   5' 11"   12st 0lbs
Born: Ansley, Warwickshire, 16 June 1903
Died: Stafford, 1 March 1983
Career: Rugeley Villa 1922. Cannock Town 1925. Sunderland March 1927. Bournemouth & Boscombe Athletic July 1928. Connah's Quay & Shotton July 1929. Southport November 1929. NELSON June1930. Hednesford Town August 1931 to 1932.
Debut v Rochdale (a) 30.8.30, lost 4–5
Charlie Dixon did not reach senior level with Sunderland, his League debut coming with Bournemouth, for whom he made 32 League and Cup appearances in 1928-29. After a season of non-League football he made 19 appearances for Southport prior to joining Nelson. In a season at Seedhill he shared centre-half duties with Jack Martin and was said to be at his best in heavy going. Particularly strong in the air, he was said to head the ball further than many of his colleagues could kick it. He would doubtless have made more than 16 appearances had he not been sent off at Carlisle United in March 1931. Carlisle won 8–1 and Dixon's severe suspension caused him to miss six matches, his return coinciding with Nelson's swansong in the Football League, a 4–0 defeat at Hull City. A part time professional throughout, Dixon additionally worked as an insurance agent. His son, Graham, was a player with Stafford Rangers from 1958 to 1962.
Appearances: FL: 16 apps 1 gl Total: 16 apps 1 gl

DIXON, Ernest 'Ernie'

Centre-forward
5' 9 ½"   12st 0lbs
Born: Pudsey, 10 July 1901
Died: Bradford, 27 April 1941
Career: Calverley. Leeds Amateurs. Bradford City August 1921. Halifax Town May 1922. Burnley March 1924, with Ben Wheelhouse and George Parkin for a combined fee of £2,000. Halifax Town December 1924. Huddersfield Town August 1929, fee £1,000. NELSON October 1929, fee £300. Tranmere Rovers August 1930. Gresley Rovers March 1933. Mossley 1933.

Debut v Hartlepools United (a) 19.10.29, won 2–1 (scored one)

A strong centre-forward of the bustling type, Ernie Dixon was a familiar figure in the Northern Section of Division Three, and was undoubtedly one of the most dangerous attack leaders of his day. He remains the highest goal scorer in Halifax Town's history, netting 132 (127 League, five FA Cup) in two separate spells at the Shay. Sadly, Halifax were unable to hang on to their prolific scorer, twice selling him for sizeable fees to balance their books. Dixon's two spells at higher level with Burnley and Huddersfield Town were not a success, and by his own high standards his return of 10 goals in 29 matches for Nelson was a disappointment. He wound up his League career in typical fashion with an excellent return of 53 goals in 83 matches for Tranmere Rovers, taking his final career aggregate figures to a most impressive 192 goals in 357 matches.

Appearances: FL: 28 apps 10 gls FAC: 1 app 0 gls Total: 29 apps 10 gl

DODSWORTH, John George

Right-half
5' 9"   11st 0lbs
Born: Darlington, 6 March 1907
Died: Darlington, March 1998
Career: Darlington March 1928. NELSON May 1928. Shildon February 1930. Crook Town August 1930 to February 1931.
Debut v New Brighton (h) 2.2.29, won 3–0

Nelson's new manager, Mr Jack English, returned to his old club, Darlington, to sign 21 year-old reserve team wing-half John Dodsworth. The new recruit had played only once for Darlington, being given a run out in the final match of season 1927-28, a 3–1 defeat at Rotherham United. One of several Darlington players and officials who were suspended by the FA for alleged irregular payments to players, Dodsworth was not available for selection until January 1929, by which stage of the season the team had a fairly settled look. Injury to captain George Wilson in February saw Dodsworth introduced for two consecutive matches, his debut versus New Brighton and a 3–1 defeat at Wrexham one week later.

Appearances: FL: 2 apps 0 gls Total: 2 apps 0 gls

DONKIN, William

Right-back
5' 10½"   11st 11lbs
Born: Annfield Plain, 22 June 1900
Died: Gateshead, October quarter 1974
Career: Twizzell United. Annfield Plain June 1921. West Stanley September 1922. Craghead United. Preston Colliery November 1923. West Stanley. Chester-le-Street. Annfield Plain June 1925. Spennymoor United September 1926. NELSON June 1928. Spennymoor United November 1928. Annfield Plain August 1929. Shildon December 1929. Blackhall Colliery Welfare December 1930.
Debut v Hartlepools United (a) 25.8.28, drawn 2–2

Spennymoor United supporters were pleased to welcome back their full-back Billy Donkin, who returned from Nelson after a brief stay, covering just eight League outings in the early months of season 1928-29. Urgent family and personal reasons were the reason for his swift return homewards, Nelson's directors dealing sympathetically with the matter and allowing him to return unconditionally. In May 1931 it was reported that Donkin was playing for Wheatley Hill Cricket Club and had a batting average of 127 runs. One of the best all-rounders ever produced in North-West Durham, numbered amongst his feats was the taking of six wickets in three overs without conceding a run. This was for Sacriston Colliery against Backworth, a Tyneside League team. He also held professional engagements with Birtley C.C. and Dean Park C.C.

Appearances: FL: 8 apps 0 gls Total: 8 apps 0 gls

EARLE, Edwin

Outside-left
5' 9 ½"   11st 0lbs
Born: North Seaton, 17 June 1905
Died: North Seaton, 22 October 1987
Career: Newbiggin Athletic. Blyth Spartans amateur July, professional November 1924. NELSON September 1925.

Burnley December 1926, fee £1,250. Boston Town July 1928. Crystal Palace July 1933. Gresley Rovers August 1934. Boston United January 1935. Wisbech Town November 1935.

Debut v Ashington (h) 15.9.25, drawn 2–2

A perceived weakness at outside-left in the early weeks of season 1925-26 led Nelson representatives to undertake a midnight trip North to sign Edwin Earle from Blyth Spartans. When the deputation arrived, Earle had just completed a night shift in the local coalmine, but played on the same day that he was signed, travelling to Nelson without having been to bed – not the best preparation for his Football League debut! Described as one of the outstanding players operating in the North-Eastern League, he did not disappoint his sponsors, the youthful wingman immediately embarking on a run of 57 League and Cup appearances. Possessing ball control, speed, and the ability to beat an opponent cleverly, Earle attracted the attention of several First Division clubs, including Aston Villa, Everton and Liverpool. Initially rejecting all overtures for his transfer, Nelson continued to benefit from his resourceful wing play and opportunism. His particularly bright start to season 1926-27 included a hat-trick in the opening home match against Doncaster Rovers, and after eight goals in 17 League matches, Burnley paid £1,250 for his transfer. Signed as understudy to England International Louis Page at outside-left, Earle lacked first team opportunities at Turf Moor and was transfer listed at £750 in the summer of 1928. He re-appeared in League football some years later with Crystal Palace and scored on his debut at Southend United in a 4–0 win in August 1933.

Appearances: FL: 54 apps 15 gls FAC: 3 apps 0 gls Total: 57 apps 15 gls

EASTWOOD, Edmund

Full-back 5' 9" 11st 6lbs
Born: Nelson, 7 January 1902
Died: Burnley, 15 July 1981
Career: Barrowford. NELSON amateur June1920, professional May 1922. Morecambe July 1923. Clitheroe June 1929. Rossendale United March 1930. Heywood St James. Darwen March 1935.

Debut v Darlington (h) 1.10.21, drawn 1–1

A local product from the Barrowford club, Eastwood was first tried in the reserve team at the beginning of season 1920-21 and assisted them to the championship of the North-East Lancashire Combination. He then made maximum appearances in the Central League side in the following season. Rewarded with a professional contract in May 1922 he added only a further two first team outings to his total before joining Morecambe in July 1923. The keen and plucky full-back enjoyed a long record of consistency with the Christie Park club, missing only a handful of matches in all seasons but his last, and this due to injury. Along with Harry Clayton (q.v.) he was a member of the 1926-27 Morecambe side that won the Lancashire Junior Cup, the Combination Cup for the first time, and finished third in the league.

Appearances: FL: 3 apps 0 gls Total: 3 apps 0 gls

EDDLESTON, Joseph

Centre-forward 5' 6 ½" 10st 6lbs
Born: Oswaldtwistle, 29 December 1896
Died: Blackburn, 24 March 1959
Career: St Mary's RC, (Oswaldtwistle). Blackburn Rovers May 1919. NELSON April 1921. Swindon Town August 1926. Accrington Stanley July 1932. Fleetwood August 1933 to May 1934.

Debut v Wigan Borough (h) 27.8.21, lost 1–2

A product of St Mary's RC, a prolific junior nursery, Joe Eddleston spent two seasons in reserve with Blackburn Rovers, yet in limited first team opportunities netted three goals in seven matches. Considering his subsequent success as a marksman, it occurs that he might have been worth persevering with at Ewood Park, although one contemporary report suggested that the Rovers considered his lack of physique for the centre-forward role a major drawback. The Rovers' loss was Nelson's gain, however, and Eddleston was quickly back into League football when Nelson became a Third Division North side just a couple of months after the bantam weight forward's arrival at Seedhill. A natural body swerve and good pace, combined with a strong shot in either foot, reaped the all-action centre-forward a rich harvest of goals. He led the scoring charts in each of his five seasons at Seedhill, averaging 20 goals a season. His best return came in 1924-25, when he scored 26 League and Cup goals in 43 matches. He was also outstanding in the 1922-23 championship season, scoring 23 goals in 36 matches. He was placed on the transfer list in May 1926 with a fee of £300 on his head, the asking price was reduced to £250 in the following month, and in August he joined Swindon Town. In six seasons with the Wiltshire side he scored 64 goals in 203 League appearances. A final move in senior football brought him homewards to Lancashire, and in a season with Accrington Stanley he scored 12 goals in 40 League appearances and recorded his 400th League appearance. Known during his Nelson days as "Little Joe", he was as quick-witted as he was nimble-footed. Always the life and soul of the party, he found a perfect foil in Harry Abbott, whom he called "Brains", which he once told him was a great compliment as goalkeepers were not supposed to have any!

Appearances: FL: 183 apps 97 gls FAC: 10 apps 3 gls Total: 193 apps 100 gls

Honours: NELSON, Third Division North champions 1923.

ELLERINGTON, William

Centre-half
5' 11"   12st 0lbs
Born: Sunderland, July quarter 1892
Died: Southampton, October quarter 1948
Career: Fatfield Albion. Darlington South Bank. Darlington FC February 1912. Wartime guest player with Southampton and Harland & Wolff. Middlesbrough May 1919, fee £30. NELSON June 1924, fee £350. Pontypridd. Mid-Rhondda August 1925. Ebbw Vale November 1925, player-manager April 1926. Basingstoke Town September 1930.
Debut v Southport (a) 30.8.24, lost 0-1

A member of the Darlington team that won the championship of the North Eastern League in season 1912-13, Bill Ellerington joined Middlesbrough for a bargain fee of £30, and completed 131 League and Cup matches in five seasons at Ayresome Park. He had played in little first team football in his final season, but commanded what was at the time a sizeable fee when he moved to Seedhill in June 1924. Nelson were intent on bouncing back from their relegation from the Second Division in the previous season, and they came very near to achieving their objective, finishing runners-up to Darlington, when only the champions were promoted. Ellerington's season was unfortunately curtailed by injury after he had performed with a polished style and tireless energy in the first 25 matches of the season, and while Ernie Braidwood moved over from left-half and proved a very effective pivot, his vacated role on the left flank was never satisfactorily filled. On leaving Nelson, aged 33, Ellerington did not reappear in League football. His son, also William, was capped by England in 1949 while on Southampton's books

Appearances: FL: 26 apps 2 gls FAC: 2 apps 0 gls Total: 28 apps 2 gls

FAIRHURST, William Shaw 'Billy'

Left-back 5' 8 ½"   12st 0lbs
Born: Blyth, 1 October 1902
Died: Middlesbrough, 27 February 1979
Career: Bebside Gordon. Blyth Spartans February 1924. Middlesbrough May 1925. Southport May 1928. NELSON July 1929. Northampton Town June 1932. Hartlepools United August 1933. Tranmere Rovers May 1935.
Debut v Southport (h) 31.8.29, drawn 2-2

Born into a family of footballers and one of ten children, Billy's father was a Blyth Spartans player, brother David was capped by England in 1934 and was an FA Cup winner with Newcastle United in 1932. A tenacious back with good powers of recovery, Billy represented the North Eastern League during Middlesbrough days, but did not appear in League football until joining Southport. He was with Nelson when they lost their Football League status, but remained at Seedhill for a season of Lancashire Combination football while working locally as a dairyman. He subsequently linked up again with former Nelson manager Jack English at Northampton Town, recording his 100th League appearances in their colours. In two seasons with Hartlepools United he made 58 League appearances, but injury blighted his final season with Tranmere Rovers. During the Second World War he served throughout hostilities with the Durham Light

Infantry and was one of the first into the infamous Belsen Concentration Camp. He subsequently worked for ICI at Billingham.
Appearances: FL: 76 apps 0 gls FAC: 4 apps 0 gls
Total: 80 apps 0 gls

FAWCETT, Desmond Hallimond

Goalkeeper
6' 0"   12st 0lbs
Born: Carlin How, Cleveland, January quarter 1905
Died: Wellington, 24 October 1968
Career: Skinnington PM Juniors. Normanby Magnesite. Loftus Albion. Middlesbrough amateur March 1923. Loftus Albion. Darlington amateur February, professional June 1926. NELSON August 1928. Preston North End August 1929. York City September 1932. Mansfield Town May 1934. Rochdale June 1936. Wellington Town May 1939.
Debut v Hartlepools United (a) 25.8.28, drawn 2–2

Said to be of retiring disposition, the former railway ticket collector enjoyed a lengthy career in League football, making his debut in Division Two with Darlington in a 1–0 home defeat by Oldham Athletic in August 1926. He cost Nelson an undisclosed fee and shared first team duties with Sam Warhurst for a season. While brilliant at times, his work was said to be of uneven quality, as he was quite capable of making 'impossible' saves, only to be beaten by a weaker shot. Despite a nightmare start of five consecutive defeats with Preston North End he remained first choice throughout his first season at Deepdale, and gave excellent service to each of his subsequent League clubs, passing the milestone of 300 League appearances with Rochdale and clocking up 70 consecutive League appearances for them between 1st January 1937 and 17th September 1938.
Appearances: FL: 23 apps 0 gls Total: 23 apps 0 gls

FERGUSON, Edward 'Ted'

Right-back   5' 9"   12st 7lbs
Born: Seaton Burn, 2 August 1895
Died: Seaton Burn, 8 February 1978
Career: Seaton Burn. Army football. Ashington June 1919. Chelsea March 1920. Ashington June 1924. NELSON August 1928. Annfield Plain August 1930. Seaton Burn Welfare amateur July 1933.
Debut v South Shields (h) 12.9.28, won 1–0

Ted Ferguson began in the North Eastern League with Ashington, and before the end of his first season his outstanding displays attracted the attention of bigger clubs, Chelsea winning the race for his signature. In a lengthy stay at Stamford Bridge he failed to break into the League side, making just two first team appearances. A return to Ashington found his old club by this time operating in the Northern Section of Division Three, and in four seasons at Portland Park he completed 121 League appearances and scored five goals. The most Northerly League club experienced their worst season financially in 1927-28, their loss in the season's working amounting to a little over £1,500. With the club still in negotiation with several players as late as August, several of the ones unsigned moved on, and Ted Ferguson joined Nelson on the 29th of the month. Despite his lack of pre-season training, the new recruit was quickly installed at right-back and for two seasons the robust and quick tackling defender

played a large part in the improved defensive qualities of a team that had conceded a staggering 136 goals in League matches in the season prior to his arrival.
Appearances: FL: 67 apps 0 gls FAC: 1 app 0 gls Total: 68 apps 0 gls

FERGUSON, Robert

Inside-left 5' 9" 11st 0lbs
Born: Seaton Burn, April quarter 1908
Career: Seaton Burn Juniors. Ashington "A" January 1926. West Bromwich Albion July 1926. Blyth Spartans August 1927. Annfield Plain August 1928. NELSON June 1929. Annfield Plain November 1929. Jarrow August 1931. Seaton Burn Welfare amateur July 1933.
Debut v Crewe Alexandra (a) 7.9.29, lost 0–4

The 1929-30 season opened disastrously for Nelson, the team made an unsuccessful start and injuries sidelined a number of players at a time when their services were urgently required. The local correspondent considered that: "The inside-forwards constitute the cardinal weakness of the side," continuing to say "The halves are not perfect, but they are run off their feet owing to the inability of the forwards to hold on to the ball." As Robert Ferguson, younger brother of Edward (q.v.), made his solitary League appearance in the 4–0 defeat at Crewe Alexandra and was returned to Annfield Plain two months later, he was obviously considered unready for Third Division football.

Appearances: FL: 1 app 0 gls Total: 1 app 0 gls

FERRARI, Frederick Joseph 'Fred'

Centre-forward 5' 8 ½" 12st 4lbs
Born: Stratford, London, 22 May 1901
Died: Sheffield, 6 August 1970
Career: Barking Town. Leyton FC. Northampton Town October 1925. Sheffield Wednesday June 1926, fee £800. Flint Town United (trial) August 1927. Norwich City December 1927, fee £150. Barrow August 1928. NELSON June 1929, fee £85. Chesterfield (trial) February 1930. Burton Town March 1930. Bedouins August 1930. Mansfield Town (trial) November 1930. Queens Park Rangers January 1931. Hillsborough Old Boys amateur September 1933. Darwin's Sports amateur October 1936.
Debut v Southport (h) 31.8.29, drawn 2–2

Fred Ferrari enjoyed his best season in League football with Barrow, his 16 goals in 28 matches including a hat-trick against Nelson in a 7–2 thrashing at Holker Street in February 1929. Not surprisingly, Nelson's directors were in pursuit of his services in the close season, but rather more puzzling was their reluctance to persevere with him after he had scored three goals in his first seven outings. Fred, whose father was Italian, settled in Sheffield where he worked in the steel industry.

Appearances: FL: 7 apps 3 gls Total: 7 apps 3 gls

FLETCHER, Jack

Outside-left 5' 6½" 11st 0lbs
Born: Padiham, 6 August 1905
Career: Colne Town. NELSON amateur October 1927; re-registering again on amateur forms May 1929. Clitheroe December 1929. Accrington Stanley amateur October 1930. Burnley amateur February 1932. Fleetwood season 1933-34.
Debut v Lincoln City (a) 29.10.27, drawn 0–0

Local amateur Jack Fletcher made his second League appearance in the wake of the humiliating 9–1 defeat at Bradford City on 12th November 1927. He had made his first appearance shortly after the transfer of Jimmy Hampson to Blackpool, but Fletcher was hardly built for the centre-forward role, and the remainder of his first team matches were at outside-left, apart from what proved to be his final appearance against Accrington Stanley, when he was fielded at outside-right. He was later to join Stanley, again on amateur forms and, on his reserve team debut, the 'Accrington Observer' optimistically considered him to be "Clever and tricky, and something of a find". He was given an early first team outing, but it coincided with the team's fifth consecutive defeat and he did not reappear in the League side.

Appearances: FL: 11 apps 1 gl FAC: 1 app 0 gls Total: 12 apps 1 gl

GARNETT, Tom

Outside-left 5' 8" 10st 5lbs
Born: Burnley, April quarter 1900
Died: Burnley, 10 January 1950
Career: NELSON amateur August 1921. By 1931 was trainer at Northwich Victoria.
Debut v Ashington (h) 14.1.22, lost 0–2

Nelson fielded a pair of amateur wingers for the visit of Ashington. With Proctor seemingly out of favour and Bennie and Eddleston laid low by a bout of influenza, Tom Garnett and Billy Wilson stepped up but neither were able to seize the opportunity in a team display that was said to be disappointing in the extreme.

Appearances: FL: 1 app 0 gls Total: 1 app 0 gls

GARTSIDE, Robert

Centre-forward 5' 7" 10st 7lbs
Born: Nelson, 21 January 1906
Died: Nelson, 26 August 1970
Career: Barnoldswick Town. Trawden FC. NELSON amateur March 1929. Clitheroe

November 1929. Bacup Borough November 1930. Clitheroe November 1931. NELSON cs 1932. Hodge House (Nelson) September 1933. St Mary's Mission (Nelson) October 1935. G. Smith's Sports Club (Colne) October 1936. NELSON trainer 1947 to 1952 and a Director from May 1957.
Debut v Barrow (h) 12.10.29, won 2–0

An injury to Gerard Kelly brought about the introduction of Bob Gartside for his Football League debut. Tom Carmedy was switched to outside-right and the local amateur newcomer brought in at centre-forward. Sadly, the 'Nelson Leader' reported that he did not enjoy a successful debut, considering that " The vast difference between Combination football and the Third Division made him appear slow and cumbersome, and he was too easily knocked off the ball, lacking the necessary physique for attack leader". Nelson won a poor game by 2–0 and in the following month Bob Gartside departed Seedhill to join Clitheroe. He returned after a season to assist his hometown club for a second spell, and in post war years became a popular sporting personality in his role as trainer, during the club's most successful period. His years with the bucket and sponge spanned two Lancashire Combination League and Cup 'doubles' in 1950 and 1951. The team were also runners-up in 1948 and in the FA Cup in season 1950-51, they progressed to Round Two before losing 3–2 at Port Vale. In addition to football, Bob Gartside spent summer months as an umpire in the Lancashire League.
Appearances: FL: 1 app 0 gls Total: 1 app 0 gls

GASKELL, Richard Halliwell

Inside-right   5' 8"   11st 0lbs
Born: Wigan, 11 October 1905
Died: Skelmersdale, 23 June 1983
Career: Wigan Borough amateur September 1926. NELSON amateur February 1928.
Westhoughton Collieries. Bolton Wanderers amateur February 1929. Darwen August 1929. Chorley 1930-31. Parbold FC 1931-32. Chorley (trial) during season 1932-33.
Debut v Durham City (a) 4.2.28, lost 0–3

Nelson cancelled the contracts of six players during January and February 1928. Earlier in the season they transferred Hampson to Blackpool and White to Walsall. The departure of these players left the club with an experimental side, as no experienced men had been signed as replacements. Richard Gaskell, an assistant head teacher at Highfields Secondary Boys' School in Wigan was just one of a number of amateur players drafted in, but the same problems persisted, insufficient penetration from the forwards and a leaky defence.
Appearances: FL: 3 apps 0 gls Total: 3 apps 0 gls

GILLAN, Felix

Centre-half
Born: Untraced
Died: Glasgow, 1986, age 82
Career: St Anthony's. Ayr United June 1925. Queen of the South. NELSON October 1928. Raith Rovers October 1929. Galston FC September 1932.
Debut v Chesterfield (a) 6.10.28, lost 2–3

Sweeping changes were the order of the day at Nelson in the summer of 1928. A determined effort was made to improve upon the dismal showing of 1927-28, when the club were obliged to seek re-election. A team manager was appointed (Mr Jack English) and only six of the previous season's players were retained. Despite the sweeping changes and a welter of new signings, defensive frailties were still apparent, and another dip into the transfer market brought Felix Gillan to Seedhill, as cover for veteran skipper, George Wilson. With his previous experience confined to Second Division football in Scotland, the new pivot took some time to adjust to League football. His best run spanned the month of December, but he was deposed after a 3–2 defeat at Ashington on New Year's Day. He made only two more first team appearances, the last of which was a comprehensive 7–2 defeat at Barrow on 23rd February 1929.
Appearances: FL: 11 apps 0 gls Total: 11 apps 0 gls

GILLIBRAND, Ernest Percival

Outside-left   5' 5"   9st 7lbs
Born: Prestwich, 27 August 1901
Died: Macclesfield, October quarter 1976
Career: Hugh Oldham Lads. Compstall. Northwich Victoria 1920-21. Glossop. Aston Villa amateur March, professional May 1922. NELSON August 1923. Rossendale United August 1924. Manchester North End October 1925. Stalybridge Celtic January 1926. Buxton September 1926. Denton United September 1927. Hyde United June 1929. Denton United May 1930. Buxton March 1931. Ashton National August 1935. Stalybridge Celtic May 1936. Droylsden September 1936. Droylsden United player-manager January 1937. Denton February 1937. Also assisted Hurst at some point.
Debut v Blackpool (a) 29.12.23, drawn 1–1

The career of Ernest Gillibrand did not lack variety and presented something of a challenge for even the most dedicated of football researchers. Pint-sized wingmen were not uncommon in inter-war football but Gillibrand's frail physique hardly fitted him for top-flight football, although he was known to have completed exactly 500 Manchester League appearances in November 1934.
Appearances: FL: 2 apps 0 gls Total: 2 apps 0 gls

HALLIGAN, William

Inside-forward
5' 8 ½"   11st 10lbs
Born: Bogginfirm, County Antrim, Ireland, 18 February 1886
Career: Old St Mary's (Dublin). Cliftonville. Belfast Celtic. Belfast Distillery August 1909. Leeds City May 1909. Derby County February 1910, fee £400. Wolverhampton Wanderers June 1911, fee £450. Hull City May 1913, fee £600. Wartime guest player with Manchester United, Rochdale, Stockport County and Chesterfield Municipal. Preston North End July 1919. Oldham Athletic January 1920, fee £750. Nelson August 1921, fee £75, retired May 1922.
Debut v Wigan Borough (h) 27.8.21, lost 1–2 (scored)

Twice capped by Ireland and an Irish League representative, William Halligan also won two Victory International caps in 1919. "A fine craftsman and a capital shot" was one early verdict, and he was certainly impressive when scoring in each of his first three matches for Nelson. Recruited from Oldham Athletic, player-manager Wilson's previous club, his signing was something of a gamble as he had not played since Christmas Day 1920. Shortly after scoring the only goal of the match for the Latics against Bradford City his season ended prematurely when he suffered a broken ankle. Despite failing to maintain a first team place during his season at Seedhill, he nevertheless netted his 100th goal in League football before announcing his retirement in the close season.

Appearances: FL: 17 apps 6 gls FAC: 3 apps 0 gls
Total: 20 apps 6 gls
Honours: Irish International, 2 caps 1911-12. Two Victory International caps 1919. One Irish League appearance versus Scottish League in 1909.

HALLIWELL, Joseph Adam

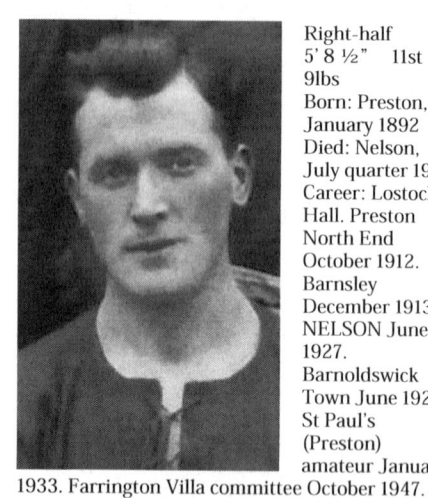

Right-half
5' 8 ½"   11st 9lbs
Born: Preston, 17 January 1892
Died: Nelson, July quarter 1964
Career: Lostock Hall. Preston North End October 1912. Barnsley December 1913. NELSON June 1927. Barnoldswick Town June 1929. St Paul's (Preston) amateur January 1933. Farrington Villa committee October 1947.
Debut v Accrington Stanley (h) 27.8.27, lost 1–4

Joe Halliwell scored his 100th League goal in Nelson's colours. He began with Preston North End as a budding centre-forward and scored 10 goals in 22 matches when North End won the Second Division championship in 1912-13. Midway through the following term he was transferred to Barnsley, and in a lengthy spell at Oakwell that spanned the First World War, he made 312 League appearances and scored 83 goals. He played in every match in his first season with Nelson, the majority from the right-half position. In the following season he had lengthy spells at centre-forward and inside-left and scored nine goals in 32 matches. Joe was later the landlord at the White Bear Hotel at Barrowford. A brother, Harry, was also with Preston North End, but did not reach first team level.

Appearances: FL: 74 apps 9 gls Total: 74 apps 9 gls
Honours: Preston North End Division Two champions 1913.

HAMPSON, James

Centre-forward 5' 7½" 11st 5lbs
Born: Little Hulton, 23 March 1906
Died: Fleetwood, 10 January 1938
Career: St John's (Little Hulton). Ogden Primitive Methodists. Walkden Park Primitive Methodists. Trials with Blackburn Rovers, Bolton Wanderers and Manchester United. NELSON amateur March, professional June 1925. Blackpool October 1927 to his death, fee £1,250.
Debut v Southport (h) 12.9.25, drawn 3–3 (scored one.)

A deadly shot with his right foot and clever in headwork, Jimmy Hampson joined Nelson at nineteen years of age and quickly proved to be an adaptable and dangerous forward with quite startling acceleration. Occupying all three inside-forward positions in his first season, he jumped into fame by scoring three hat-tricks within the space of four matches in mid term. When Joe Eddleston was transferred to Swindon Town in August 1926, Hampson took over the role of attack leader with outstanding success, netting 25 League and Cup goals in 37 matches. He had scored six goals in nine matches at the start of season 1927-28 when the inevitable happened, Nelson reluctantly agreeing to sell their prized asset to Blackpool for the then significant fee of £1,250. Unsurprisingly, Nelson had to apply for re-election at the end of the season. Jimmy Hampson, meanwhile, scored on his debut for Blackpool and netted 31 goals in just 32 League matches in his first season. It was a pattern repeated throughout his career at Bloomfield Road, and to this day he holds the club record for most League goals in total aggregate (246), and highest League scorer in a season (45). He also scored five goals in Blackpool's joint record victory, 7–0 against Reading in November 1928. His 45 goals in 1929-30 took Blackpool into the First Division for the first time. He was unfortunate to be around when 'Dixie' Dean was England's star centre-forward, but Hampson did win three caps, scoring five goals, and he represented the Football League on four occasions, scoring nine goals. Despite his outstanding contribution to Blackpool's cause, in May 1933 it was reported that he had not come to terms with the club's officials who had effectively offered him a reduction in wages. The difficulty centred on a serious 'cut' if he was not playing in the first team. Matters were subsequently resolved and Hampson remained a Blackpool player right up to the time of his tragic death in a boating accident, at the age of 31. The yacht in which he was sailing was involved in a collision with a trawler off Fleetwood and his body was never recovered. Jimmy Hampson was a former collier who played cricket and liked a game of billiards and, in addition to his football career, was also employed as a salesman in a Blackpool gent's outfitters. His brother, Harold, was an inside-forward who appeared in League football with Southport and Sheffield United in the 1930s.

Appearances: FL: 64 apps 42 gls FAC: 2 app 2 gls
Total: 66 apps 44 gls
Honours: England International, 3 caps, 1931-33. Football League representative, 4 appearances. Blackpool: Division Two champions 1930.

HARGREAVES, Harold 'Harry'

Inside-left
5' 10"   11st 10lbs
Born: Higham, 15 March 1896. No date of death found.
Career: Higham. Great Harwood October 1914. Leeds City (trial) 1915. Army football (East Lancashire Regiment). NELSON season 1919-20, registered for FL matches August 1921. Wolverhampton Wanderers November 1921, fee £1,200. Pontypridd June 1923. Tottenham Hotspur December 1923. Burnley March1926, fee £1,200. Rotherham United May 1928. Rossendale United October 1930. Barnoldswick Town March 1931. Nelson Town October 1936. NELSON Committee June 1946.
Debut v Wigan Borough (h) 27.8.21, lost 1–2

At the tender age of 17, Harry Hargreaves had reached Lancashire Combination status with Great Harwood, and attracted the interest of the great Herbert Chapman, then manager of Leeds City. He played in trials alongside Ivan Sharpe, the England amateur outside-left, who was later a well-known critic, author, and commentator for the BBC. The Great War halted his progress, but he served with distinction, reaching the rank of sergeant, being wounded and suffering as a prisoner of war for eighteen months. He began with Nelson after the war, and in two seasons of Central League football scored 34 goals, four of them coming in one match against Stockport County Reserves in a 7–0 win in December 1920. Three goals in his first two League matches for Nelson earned him a big-money move to Wolverhampton Wanderers, but he was released after scoring just eight goals in 53 League matches. He joined Pontypridd of the Welsh League and was said to have scored 49 goals at the time of his mid season transfer to Tottenham Hotspur. Life in the First Division proved difficult and he scored only seven goals in 34 League matches before moving on to Burnley. In his first full season at Turf Moor he seriously injured his knee at Sunderland on 6th October, and it was not until 19th March that he made a scoring return in a 2–1 home win against West Bromwich Albion. He scored his last League goal, before a crowd of 32,441 spectators, in the opening First Division fixture of season 1927-28, the local 'Derby' against Blackburn Rovers at Ewood Park that ended in a 2–1 victory for the home side. After returning to Lancashire Combination football, the final glimpse of his playing career saw him assisting Nelson Town, in the local amateur league. In addition to his talents as a footballer, as a young amateur cricketer with Railway Street Wesleyans he created a record in the Padiham League by winning in one season the prize for the best batting average, for the best bowling average and the best fielding prize. In later years he turned to bowls and won numerous awards in local competitions. In post WW2 years, Harry became a director of the re-born Nelson club. He later ran a fish and chip shop close to Burnley's ground. From earliest years he was known by the unlikely nickname 'Pey', the source of which is unknown.
Appearances: FL: 13 apps 2 gls Total: 13 apps 2 gls

HARKER, Willie

Inside-right   5' 8"   11st 2lbs
Born: Brierfield, 21 December 1910
Died: Oswaldtwistle, 3 July 1973
Career: West Lancashire League football. Burnley amateur May 1929. NELSON amateur August 1930. Burnley May 1931. Torquay United June 1933. Accrington Stanley June 1934. Portsmouth February 1936, along with Bob Mortimer for a combined fee of £1,450. Stockport County September 1936. Rochdale June 1939. Wartime guest player with Accrington Stanley.
Debut v Southport (a) 1.1.31, lost 1–8

The son of a Burnley publican, Willie entered the licensed trade himself when his playing days ended. His introduction to League football was not an easy one, as he came into a Nelson side in terminal decline. Despite being on the wrong end of an 8–1 score line on his debut the young inside-forward held his place for 17 consecutive matches and at the close of the season he made the short journey to Turf Moor, where he made 27 League appearances and scored seven goals in two years with Burnley. Subsequent spells in the south of England were not a success, his most productive period coming with Accrington Stanley. On 16th November 1935, he broke the club's individual scoring record by netting five goals in the 6–1 defeat of Gateshead. He scored three in six minutes and four in ten minutes, and the club presented him with the match ball. Rather ironically, an own-goal by Harker helped Accrington Stanley to a 3–2 win against Stockport County in the last League match before World War Two. After retiring from football, he became licensee of the Hare and Hounds Inn, Blackburn Road, West End, Oswaldtwistle.

Appearances: FL: 18 apps 5 gls Total: 18 apps 5 gls

HARPER, William 'Billy'

Right-back   6' 0"   11st 7lbs
Born: Blackburn, 17 August 1897
Died: Blackpool, 20 January 1982
Career: Feniscowles. NELSON amateur August, professional December 1924. Darwen May 1925. Chorley May 1927.
Debut v Lincoln City (a) 18.3.25, lost 1–2

Billy Harper was recommended to Nelson's directors by Billy Williams, a former Blackpool player. He was living at Feniscowles at the time and playing in the Blackburn Amateur League. A cool defender, strong in the tackle, he deputised for Bob Lilley with some success in six matches in March and April 1925. Harper's fourth outing, the April fixture against Darlington, attracted a 'gate' of approximately 13,500, and record Seedhill receipts of £678. The match was drawn 1–1, Darlington going on to win the championship of the Northern Section, Nelson finishing as runners-up.

Appearances: FL: 6 apps 0 gls Total: 6 apps 0 gls

HARRIS, Ambrose

Half-back
5' 7"   10st 5lbs
Born: Harle Syke, 29 October 1902
Died: Harle Syke, July quarter 1952
Career: Briercliffe. NELSON August 1924 to May 1928. Barnoldswick Town. Brierfield Central October 1931.
Debut v Chesterfield (h) 25.12.24, won 1–0

A most capable utility half-back who enjoyed extended runs of first team football in seasons 1925-26 and 1926-27. Although lightly built he was a clever dribbler and perceptive passer, and his two-footed ability enabled him to play at either right or left-half. In season 1925-26 he took over the left-half position from Ernie Braidwood from December onwards. Earlier in the same season he had assisted the reserve team to get off to a flying start, on their way to winning the Lancashire Combination championship.

Appearances: FL: 58 apps 1 gl Total: 58 apps 1 gl

HARTLEY, Roy

Right-half   5' 7½"   10st 0lbs
Born: Brierfield, 6 January 1897
Died: Staincliffe, October 1984
Career: NELSON amateur July 1919, registered for FL matches June 1921.
Debut v Stalybridge Celtic (a) 27.12.21, lost 0–2

Four League matches within the space of eight days over the Christmas/New Year period in season 1921-22 stretched Nelson's playing resources, and the visit to Stalybridge Celtic showed a number of team changes that included League debuts for Roy Hartley, and a second senior outing for goalkeeper Harry Clegg. Although Nelson had beaten Stalybridge by a goal to nil at Seedhill in their first meeting, the return fixture was pretty much "one-way traffic" and Nelson were considered fortunate to have escaped a heavier defeat than 2–0. Roy Hartley was the fifth son of Watson Hartley, a cotton weaver.

Appearances: FL: 1 app 0 gls Total: 1 app 0 gls

HAWES, Arthur Robert

Inside-left
5' 9"   11st 0lbs
Born: Swanton Morley, Norfolk, 2 October 1895
Died: Norwich, 11 October 1963
Career: Thorpe Hamlet School. Junior Institute. Norwich CEYMS. Boulton & Paul's FC. Norwich City September 1915. Norfolk County. South Shields May 1920. Sunderland December 1921, fee £1,750. Bradford Park Avenue August 1927, fee £650. Accrington Stanley July 1929, fee £100. NELSON July 1930, fee £50. Hyde United August 1931. Wombwell December 1931. Rochdale February 1932. Goole Town August 1932. Frost's Athletic July 1935. Gothic trainer to 1958, Vice-Chairman 1961.
Debut v Hull City (a) 2.9.30, lost 0–2
The son of a long serving Norwich City assistant trainer, Arthur had a thorough grounding in the area's junior football prior to joining the club. A reputation for goal scoring was enhanced with City – he scored 79 in wartime friendly matches, a total that included seven hat-tricks. An accomplished one and a half seasons with South Shields attracted a big money move to Sunderland, and he heralded his arrival at Roker Park by scoring twice in a 5–0 victory against West Bromwich Albion. His progress was such that he appeared in an England trial match (for the Rest v England in February 1925). He later won a Third Division North championship medal with Bradford Park Avenue in 1928, but his season with Nelson ended prematurely when he was injured in late February. His final League club was Rochdale, whose ranks he joined in his 37th year. An idiosyncrasy was the carrying of a handkerchief in his left hand throughout a match.
Appearances: FL: 26 apps 3 gls FAC: 3 apps 1 gl Total: 29 apps 4 gls
Honours: Bradford Park Avenue, Third Division North champions 1928.

HAYES, Thomas George

Inside or Centre-forward   5' 9"   11st 6lbs
Born: Port Talbot, 25 September 1909
Died: Port Talbot, 16 May 1984
Career: Wales Schoolboys. Port Talbot. Bridgend Town. Barnsley August 1927. NELSON March to May 1928.
Debut v Hartlepools United (a) 17.3.28, won 5–4
A number of late season signings, in a bid to avoid a re-election application, included George Hayes, an inside or centre-forward with no previous senior experience. Early signs were promising, although the new recruit was said to lack match fitness. On the credit side, he proved to have a powerful shot and the ability to hold the ball while awaiting support. Five goals in nine matches was a worthy effort, but the team's failings were mainly in defence. In the last four matches, when an escape from the bottom two places was a possibility, the team scored eleven goals but conceded fifteen and took only two points, finishing at the foot of the table.
Appearances: FL: 9 apps 5 gls Total: 9 apps 5 gls

HEDLEY, Foster

Outside-left
5' 7"   10st 10lbs
Born: Monkseaton, 6 January 1908
Died: Wembley, 22 December 1983
Career: Stanhope Road School. St Andrew's (Newcastle). South Shields. Corinthians (Newcastle). Jarrow. Hull City May 1928. NELSON May 1929. Manchester City March 1930. Chester July 1931. Tottenham Hotspur November 1933. Millwall June 1937. Swindon Town April 1939. Wartime guest player with Reading. Retired September 1946.
Debut v Southport (h) 31.8.29, drawn 2–2
Foster Hedley had played only twice for Hull City in his season at Boothferry Park, but he developed remarkably well during his ten months with Nelson. Although not always well supported he showed skill and speed and the ability to beat an opponent in very little space. Snapped up by Manchester City as understudy to Eric Brook – who went on to make nearly 500 appearances for the Maine Road club – Hedley played just twice, despite scoring in both matches. The most successful spell of his career followed, as he scored 29 goals in 88 League matches for Chester. In January 1933 he scored seven goals within the

space of a week. Four goals against Fulham in a 3rd round FA Cup-tie being followed by a hat-trick against Accrington Stanley. In the same year he assisted Chester to win the Welsh Cup. Despite a stay approaching four years at White Hart Lane, Hedley played in only four League matches for Spurs. With Millwall for two seasons, he scored four goals in eight matches in 1937-38 as the Lions won the championship of the Third Division South, he also represented the Southern League versus the Cheshire County League in October 1937. His spell with Swindon Town was curtailed by the outbreak of the Second World War. His career aggregate figures were 43 goals in 139 League matches for seven clubs.
Appearances: FL: 26 apps 5 gls FAC: 1 app 0 gls
Total: 27 apps 5 gls

HEPWORTH, Arthur

Left-half 5' 9½" 11st 10lbs
Born: Barnsley, 28 February 1908
Died: Mirfield, February 1988
Career: Worsborough Communion, St Luke's Church. Dodsworth and Yorkshire Schoolboys. Barnsley October 1926. NELSON March 1928. Wombwell August 1929. E & A Smith's Sports (Cleckheaton) amateur September 1931. Battyford Wanderers (Mirfield) amateur October 1933. Wartime guest player with Lincoln City 1943-44.
Debut v Hartlepools United (h) 17.3.28, won 5–4
The son of Walter, a former Barnsley player, Arthur Hepworth continued the family tradition when he joined the Oakwell staff at the age of eighteen. Very much a footballing family, Arthur's son, Ronald, made over a century of League appearance for Bradford Park Avenue in the immediate post war years. Arthur was signed by Nelson from Barnsley, along with George Hayes (q.v.), in the late stages of season 1928-29. Although without senior experience he was said to play "Fearlessly and smartly" and despite a nervous start on his debut, he quickly settled, and had done enough in ten matches to earn a contract for the following season. An influx of new signings in the close season included experienced wing-halves Metcalfe (ex Preston North End) and Suttie (ex Blackburn Rovers) and Arthur Hepworth spent much of his final season in reserve.
Appearances: FL: 16 apps 0 gls Total: 16 apps 0 gls

HEYES, Henry 'Harry'

Goalkeeper
5' 10"   10st 11lbs
Born: Bolton, January quarter 1894
Died: St Helens, 12 May 1949
Career: Westhoughton. Chorley cs 1914. Coppull. Represented the Royal Flying Corps during WW1. Horwich RMI. NELSON during season 1920-21, registered for FL matches August 1921. Chorley June 1922.
Debut v Wigan Borough (h) 27.8.21, lost 1–2
Harry Heyes was one of nine players retained by Nelson at the close of season 1920-21, and the Bolton-born custodian was generally first choice during the first season of Football League action at Seedhill. A clean and safe handler he was fully capable of the occasional 'impossible' save, and comfortably held off the challenge of Robert Bruce for the first team jersey. He embarked on a second spell with Chorley after leaving Seedhill and assisted them to win the Lancashire Combination championship for the second time since the war in season 1922-23.
Appearances: FL: 26 apps 0 gls Total: 26 apps 0 gls

HIGGINBOTHAM, Henry B. 'Harry'

Inside-right
5' 11"   12st 7lbs
Born: Ashfield, NSW, Australia, 27 July 1894
Died: Springburn, Glasgow, 3 June 1950
Career: Kilsyth Rangers. Petershill. During the WW1 period assisted Hibernian, St Mirren, Third Lanark, Fulham and Millwall. South Shields July 1919. Luton Town 1920. Clapton Orient February 1923.
NELSON February 1924. Reading April 1924. Mid Rhondda 1925. Pontypridd.
Debut v Bury (a) 23.2.23, lost 0–2
A late-season signing by Nelson when all hopes of survival in Division Two were fading fast. Australian born former Scottish Junior International Harry Higginbotham failed to impress on his debut at Bury, and was similarly

43

ineffective in the following week when Manchester United won 2–0 at Seedhill. At this point, Nelson had lost six straight League matches and had not scored a single goal in any of them whilst conceding 15. The return match with Manchester United at Old Trafford was the unlikely setting for Nelson's first away victory of the season. Overplayed for much of the game, Nelson went ahead after 19 minutes through Crawshaw, and a magnificent defence, marshalled by player-manager David Wilson, held out for a famous victory. United finished with ten men after full-back Charlie Radford was sent off for a bad foul on Joe Eddleston towards the end of the game. The normally hard-to-please correspondent of the 'Nelson Leader' warmly congratulated the whole side on their first away victory, and had a special word for the Scotsman: "Higginbotham in particular improved out of all recognition, and showed much versatility." He did not stay to build on his reputation, however, leaving Seedhill after the briefest of stays to join Reading for his final spell in senior football. His career figures in the Football League were 134 matches and 30 goals, his best spell coming with Luton Town (80 matches and 26 goals).

Appearances: FL: 4 apps 0 gls Total: 4 apps 0 gls

HILLAM, Charles Emmanuel

Goalkeeper 5' 11 ½" 11st 8lbs
Born: Burnley, 6 October 1908
Died: North Walsham, April 1958
Career: Bury Schoolboys. Burnley Social Democratic Federation XI. Clitheroe August 1931. Burnley amateur (trial). NELSON amateur August 1930 to January 1931, re-registered amateur March 1931. Clitheroe. Burnley May 1932. Manchester United May 1933. Clapton Orient May 1934. Southend United June 1938. Chingford Town after WW2, appointed trainer season 1948-49.
Debut v Barrow (a) 11.4.31, lost 1–2
Three matches in Nelson's final season in the Football League was Charlie Hillam's introduction to senior football, and the former collier subsequently worked hard to establish himself, being mainly a reserve team player with both Burnley (19 matches) and Manchester United (8 matches). Along with a Manchester United team-mate, Tom Manns, he travelled south to join Clapton Orient in May 1934. Hillam was again cast in a reserve role at Lea Bridge Road and had to wait nine months before being promoted to the first team. He certainly grasped his belated opportunity, however, embarking on a run of 116 consecutive League games. His senior career ended with Southend United, his final appearances coming in the abortive season 1939-40.

Appearances: FL: 3 apps 0 gls Total: 3 apps 0 gls

HOAD, Sydney James

Outside-right 5' 7½" 10st 5lbs
Born: Eltham, 27 December 1890
Died: Whitefield, 1 January 1973
Career: St Annes. Blackpool amateur December 1909. Manchester City amateur May 1911. Wartime guest player with Tottenham Hotspur and Scotswood. Rochdale September 1920. NELSON January 1922. Hurst October 1927.
Debut v Hartlepools United (h) 21.1.22, lost 0–4
The fee that Nelson paid for Syd Hoad was not disclosed, but it was said to be the highest paid by Nelson at that time. A player of ripe experience at 32 years of age, he gave Nelson excellent service throughout his five years at Seedhill. "Very smart in footwork and centres splendidly" was one verdict, another rated him as "One of the fastest wingers in the Third Division". (His father, Joseph, was a greyhound trainer, and one wonders whether he was also responsible for his son's turn of speed!). He began with Blackpool at 17 years of age and became their first international player when he was capped at

amateur level by England in 1910-11, playing against Wales, Belgium and France. Training as a lawyer while playing his football as an amateur, he nevertheless earned an upward move to First Division Manchester City, for whom he appeared in 69 League and Cup matches before the Great War. In September 1920 he joined Rochdale, at that time operating in the Central League. In the following term he made his debut in the newly formed Division Three North, moving in mid season to join Nelson, where he won a championship medal in season 1922-23. In later years he was, quite unusually, an abstemious and non-smoking licensee in Lancaster. His overall career figures for his four League clubs totalled 272 League and Cup matches and 20 goals.

Appearances: FL: 152 apps 13 gls FAC: 5 apps 0 gls Total: 157 apps 13 gls

Honours: England Amateur International, 3 caps 1910-11. NELSON, Division Three North champions 1923.

HOOPER, Alexander 'Alec'

Left-back 5' 11 ½"   12st 4lbs
Born: Darlington, 5 January 1900
Died: Burnley, October quarter 1978
Career: Shildon. Charlton Athletic July 1925. St Johnstone November 1926. NELSON June 1928. Bangor City December 1928. Barnoldswick Town August 1929. Bangor City December 1929. Accrington Stanley June 1930. Barnoldswick Town August 1930.
Debut v Hartlepools United (a) 25.8.28, drawn 2–2

Alec Hooper's senior career got off to an uncertain start, Charlton Athletic being obliged to seek re-election to the Football League for the only time in the club's history. He had appeared in seven League and two FA Cup matches during his spell at the Valley. He joined Nelson after two seasons spent in Scottish Second Division football, but he quickly lost out to his namesake, Harry Hooper, for the left-back position and was released in mid season. A third attempt to establish himself in League football with Accrington Stanley brought only a season of reserve team football.

Appearances: FL: 9 apps 0 gls Total: 9 apps 0 gls

HOOPER, Harry Reed

Full-back
5' 10" 11st 6lbs
Born: Burnley, 16 December 1910
Died: Halifax, 24 March 1970
Career: Nelson Schoolboys. Nelson Tradesmen. NELSON amateur October, professional November 1928. Sheffield United February 1930, along with Harry Tordoff for a combined fee of £750. Wartime guest player with Portsmouth, Hartlepools United and Huddersfield Town. Hartlepools United July 1947. West Ham United trainer November 1949. Halifax Town manager October 1957 to April 1962.
Debut v Carlisle United (a) 20.8.28, lost 0–4

Very much the local boy who made good, Harry Hooper shone briefly in a poor Nelson side and went on to enjoy a lengthy career as both player and manager. Discovered playing with the local Tradesman's club, he became a professional at 18 years of age. The former tailor's cutter was a quick and cool defender with a biting tackle and was an expert from the penalty spot. He joined Sheffield United, along with Harry Tordoff, and made his debut in a 5–1 win against Blackpool on Boxing Day 1930. He suffered a broken leg at Wolverhampton Wanderers on 1st October 1932 but made a complete recovery and captained the Blades in the 1936 FA Cup Final and totalled 292 League and Cup appearances (11 goals). After serving in the RAOC during the Second World War he was mainly in reserve at Bramhall Lane in post war football, but a final spell with Hartlepools United took his career total of League matches to 356. He subsequently moved to West Ham United as trainer, where his son, also Harry, was a winger who won England 'B' and Under-23 honours and represented the Football League, scoring 108 League goals in 328 matches for four different clubs.

Appearances: FL: 21 apps 0 gls Total: 21 apps 0 gls
Honours: Sheffield United, FA Cup finalists 1936.

HOWARTH, Archibald 'Archie'

Outside-left
5' 8"   11st 0lbs
Born: Bury, January quarter 1911
Died: Heywood, 20 July 1966
Career: NELSON amateur September 1930. Great Harwood December 1930.
Debut v Darlington (h) 6.9.30, won 3–1 (scored one)

One of a number of amateur players who assisted Nelson in their final season in the Third Division North, Archie Howarth began brightly, the fleet footed wingman netting on his debut and again, just four days later, in the 2–1 defeat against Lincoln City. A string of poor results eventually saw him replaced by Henry Robinson, and in the following month he requested his release and joined Great Harwood. In later years he was mine host at the Victoria Hotel, Bury.

Appearances: FL: 8 apps 2 gls Total: 8 apps 2 gls

HOWES, George Albert

Right-half   5'10 ½"   12st 0lbs
Born: Jarrow, 5 January 1906
Died: Gosforth, Newcastle-on-Tyne, 31 July 1993
Career: Jarrow. Barnsley May 1928. NELSON May 1930. Tunbridge Wells Rangers July 1931.
Debut v Rochdale (a) 30.8.30, lost 4–5

Considering his lack of senior experience on arrival at Seedhill, George Howes formed part of a fairly settled middle line comprising himself at right-half, Jack Martin as pivot and David Suttie on the left flank. After a shaky start in his first League appearance at Rochdale, he eventually won back his first team place in mid October, and was ever-present for the remainder of the season.

Appearances: FL: 35 apps 0 gls FAC: 3 apps 0 gls Total: 38 apps 0 gls

HOWSON, Charles

Right-back
5' 11"   13st 7lbs
Born: Wombwell, 18 July 1896
Died: Wombwell, July quarter 1976
Career: Rotherham Town August 1919. Wombwell 1920-21. NELSON (trial) May 1922. Port Vale (trial) November 1922. Mansfield Town December 1922 to cs 1923.
Debut v Ashington (h) 7.10.22, lost 1–3

Charlie Howson, a tall, well-built defender, was the subject of several enquiries from Football League clubs before Nelson signed him from Wombwell of the Midland League. He failed, however, to earn an extension to his trial period at Seedhill after appearing in just one League match, in which Nelson were unexpectedly beaten. Having previously won all home matches without conceding a goal, the 3–1 defeat by Ashington was a great disappointment to a large crowd, who paid £351 at the gate. Howson was introduced as Clem Rigg had been injured the previous week at Southport and remained unfit. In giving the newcomer his chance, Lilley was moved to left-back, but the experiment was not a success. Lilley appearing lost in his unaccustomed role, while Howson, according to the 'Nelson Leader's' correspondent, "failed to do his powers full justice".

Appearances: FL: 1 app 0 gls Total: 1 app 0 gls

HUMPHREY, Douglas Vincent

Outside-left   5' 6"   10st 7lbs
Born: Eccleshall Bierley, 27 September 1897
Died: Sheffield, 8 June 1965
Career: Bradford Park Avenue September 1920. Stockport County May 1922. NELSON January 1924, in exchange for Bob Hutchinson. Selby Town November 1926.
Debut v South Shields (h) 2.2.24, lost 0–2

At the outset of his career, when mainly playing in reserve team football, the slightly built wingman saw his Bradford Park Avenue team suffer successive relegations, from Division One in 1920-21 and from Division Two a year later. Moving on to Stockport County for season 1922-23, he was a key figure in their narrow escape from relegation from Division Two. Late season goals against Derby County in a 2–1 win and another in the dramatic 3–0 victory, achieved on the last day of the season against Southampton, took County to safety, one point ahead of Rotherham County who, along with Wolverhampton Wanderers, were relegated. After the opening six matches of the following campaign, Humphrey lost his first team place, reappearing just once in a 2–0 FA Cup defeat at Norwich City on December 15th. Joining Nelson in the following month, in an exchange deal that took Bob Hutchinson to Edgeley Park, the unfortunate wingman was again involved in a desperate scrap against relegation. In what proved to be his final eight appearances in League football, Humphrey featured in a winning side only once, and Nelson's sojourn in Division Two was ended.

Appearances: FL: 8 apps 0 gls Total: 8 apps 0 gls

HUTCHINSON, Robert 'Bobby'

Outside-left
5' 8½"   11st 9lbs
Born: Gosforth, 22 December 1894
Died: Gosforth, July quarter 1971
Career: Gosforth. Palmer's (Jarrow). St Mirren August 1914. Wartime guest player with Ashington January 1915. Newcastle United amateur January, professional May 1919. Ashington May 1920. NELSON May 1922. Stockport County January 1924, in exchange for Doug Humphrey. Chesterfield May 1924. Barrow July 1925. In season 1926-27 played in the USA and assisted New Bedford Whalers, Springfield Babes, Fall River Marksmen and Newark Skeeters. In 1927-28 played in eleven matches with Hartford Americans. Darlington March 1928. West Stanley September 1928. Gosforth & Coxledge BL amateur September 1930.
Debut v Bradford Park Avenue (a) 26.8.22, lost 2–6

A winger of sound experience with excellent ball control, Bobby Hutchinson could show his heels to most full-backs and centre splendidly on the run. If he had a fault, it surrounded his occasional tendency to try to beat three or four men, with the inevitable result. The undoubted highlight of his varied and nomadic career came with Nelson, where he made the maximum number of appearances in the 1922-23 championship winning side. The Geordie wingman was a great practical joker, one story surrounded his snaffling the match ball and taking it with him into the away dressing room. An official of the home club, who had seen him do it, following into the dressing room angrily demanding the return of the ball, saying that nobody would be allowed to leave until he got it. All protested their innocence including Hutchinson, who was splashing happily in the bath, and a high and low search failed to produce the missing ball. Eventually the official left the dressing room apparently completely mystified, whereupon the villain of the piece threw the ball out of the bath, where he had been sitting on it during the time that the search was carried out. Earlier in his career, Bobby did not reach senior level with Newcastle United, beginning in senior football with Ashington (23 matches and four goals). He had completed exactly a century of League appearances when he joined Barrow in July 1925 and was one of their most consistent performers (37 League appearances and four goals). He then spent two years in American football and was still turning out in non-League football in his 36th year.

Appearances: FL: 60 apps 1 gl FAC: 4 apps 0 gls
Total: 64 apps 1 gl
Honours: NELSON: Division Three North champions 1923.

JACQUES, Thomas Edgar

Half-back
5'10 ½"   11st 12lbs
Born: Skipton, 13 November 1890
Died: Nelson, October quarter 1968
Career: Victoria Cross. Blackburn Trinity. Mill Hill Woodfold. Accrington Stanley. Darwen. Blackburn Trinity 1911-12. Blackburn Rovers March 1912. NELSON July 1919, registered for FL matches August 1921. Great Harwood 1922. Barnoldswick Park Villa August 1923. Earby FC January-May 1924.
Debut v Wigan Borough (a) 3.9.21, won 4–1 (scored one)

Edgar Jacques played in just two League matches for Blackburn Rovers prior to joining the Army in 1915. He then captained his battalion team (The 6th Connaught Rangers) for over two years in France. He was taken prisoner of war and was eventually released – happily on his birthday – on November 13th, 1918, and joined Nelson in the following year. The bulk of his matches were made in the two seasons prior to Football League entry, and in 1921-22 he lost his first team place to Jimmy Price, when the Scots pivot was signed from Airdrieonians in mid season. After spells in non-League and local football, Jacques returned to Seedhill as assistant trainer and groundsman in June 1925 and was promoted to the position of first team trainer from July 1926, serving until the summer of 1928.

Appearances: FL: 17 apps 1 gl FAC: 3 apps 0 gls
Total: 20 apps 1 gl

JEWELL, John

Outside-right
Born: Brierfield, October quarter 1909
Career: Colne Town. Burnley amateur. NELSON amateur December 1930. Bacup Borough November 1932.
Debut v Wrexham (h) 20.12.30, won 2–0

Five matches that had yielded just a single point prompted Nelson's directors to make a number of

47

team changes for Wrexham's visit to Seedhill, and an all-round improvement ensued. Five different outside-rights had already been tried, and Jewell, a local wingman from Brierfield, became the sixth to occupy the problem position. The ground was partially under water, conditions deplorable for an untried player to encounter, but Jewell gave a promising display in the 2–0 victory, and was considered by the 'Nelson Leader' to be worthy of an extended run in the side. In the event, he played only twice more in the League side, but as he finished twice on the winning side in his three outings, he could be considered unfortunate to be overlooked in a season when the team won only six of their 42 League engagements.
Appearances: FL: 3 apps 0 gls Total: 3 apps 0 gls

JONES, Arthur

Left-back 5' 8 ½"   10st 7lbs
Born: Birmingham
Career: Heywood. NELSON amateur May, professional October 1927 to May 1928.
Debut v Durham City (a) 4.2.28, lost 0–3
Arthur Jones did not have a happy debut in League football. His lack of experience was exposed at Durham City when, with the match just 12 minutes old, his miss kick let in Pearson, Durham's centre-forward, who gave Nelson's goalkeeper, Sam Warhust, no chance. The same player broke away just before the interval, outwitted Jones, and registered a second goal. The 3–0 defeat left Nelson third from the bottom of the table and sadly matters did not improve as they finished at the foot of the table and were obliged to seek re-election.
Appearances: FL: 1 app 0 gls Total: 1 app 0 gls

JONES, John William 'Jack'

Left-back
5' 9"   11st 6lbs
Born: Parkgate, Rotherham, 8 February 1891
Died: Rotherham, 20 July 1948
Career: Alma Road School. Allerton Bywater Colliery. Industry FC. Bird-in-Hand FC. Maltby Main Colliery. Sunderland November 1914. Birmingham May 1920. NELSON July 1927 to February 1928. Crewe Alexandra March 1928. Scarborough September 1930. Retired May 1931.
Debut v Accrington Stanley (h) 27.8.27, lost 1–4

The 'Topical Times' magazine of April 1st, 1922 commented on the much improved form of Jack Jones, Birmingham's sturdily-built full-back: "He has risen to the full realisation of his responsibilities while Womack has been out of the side through injury. His defence in recent weeks has been splendid, and he shirks nothing and fears no one. He has made the position quite secure. There have been times when he lacked finesse and judgment, while when once beaten he also betrayed a lack of speed. But in recent games he has been invaluable. This is the kind of man that you like to have on your side." Some five years, and 228 League appearances later, Jack Jones arrived at Seedhill. Sadly, he never showed his true form in Nelson's colours and was allowed to leave in February of his only season "Unhonoured and unsung" according to the local correspondent. He was quickly back in harness with Crewe Alexandra, where his form and confidence returned. In a little over two seasons he made 91 League appearances and scored seven goals. During the First World War he served with the Royal Field Artillery.
Appearances: FL: 12 apps 0 gls FAC: 1 app 0 gls Total: 13 apps 0 gls
Honours: Football League representative, one appearance 1925. Birmingham, Division Two champions 1921.

KEERS, John Mandell

Outside-left
5' 6"   11st 0lbs
Born: Tow Law, 6 March 1901
Died: Hyde, Cheshire, 5 January 1963
Career: Chopwell Colliery. Langley Park amateur August 1924. Tow Law Town amateur November 1924. Hull City May 1925. Annfield Plain July 1926. NELSON December 1926, fee £150. Boston Town July 1927. Hyde United July 1929. Retired 1938.
Debut v Wrexham (h) 1.1.27, won 3–0
The transfer of Edwin Earle to Burnley in December 1926 brought Nelson a welcome, four-figure cash injection, but it also left a vacancy at outside-left that proved difficult to fill. Bargain signing John Keers was said to please everyone on his first appearance, despite operating in strange surroundings. In a run of eight consecutive League outings he collected six

winning bonuses and scored three goals, but he lost out when Nelson entered the transfer market in March of the same season, signing outside-left Lewis Bedford and inside-forward Harry White from Walsall. In earlier days, Keers assisted Tow Law Town to win the Northern League championship, but his record at Hull City – 8 appearances and one goal – was not dissimilar to his record with Nelson.
Appearances: FL: 8 apps 3 gls Total: 8 apps 3 gls

KELLY, Gerard

Outside-right 5' 7 ½" 11st 4lbs
Born: Hylton, Sunderland, 15 September 1909
Died: Ellesmere Port, February 1986
Career: Castletown FC. Hylton Colliery. Sunderland November 1927. NELSON June 1928. Huddersfield Town October 1929, fee £2,000. Charlton Athletic March 1932, fee £600. Chester December 1932, fee £285. Port Vale June 1936. Southampton September 1937 to 1939. Wartime guest player with Shrewsbury Town and Wrexham.
Debut v Hartlepools United (a) 25.8.28, drawn 2–2

Signed from Sunderland as a 19 year-old, Gerry Kelly had won sprinting honours as a schoolboy and scored 13 goals in as many matches for Sunderland reserves in season 1927-28. He was Nelson's outstanding forward throughout his stay at Seedhill. A brilliant winger, if inclined at times to be a little selfish, he was the scorer of some spectacular solo goals and he earned Nelson a hefty, and very welcome, fee of £2,000 when First Division Huddersfield Town moved in for his signature in October 1929. Gerry began at Leeds Road as understudy to Alex Jackson the Scottish international star wingman, and seven goals in 14 matches in his first season was an excellent start. Despite limited opportunities, he scored 15 goals in 37 League matches before moving on to Charlton Athletic. His best subsequent spell was with Chester for whom he scored 27 goals in 73 matches. His final aggregate figures were 67 goals in 218 matches, his League career ending with the outbreak of World War Two.
Appearances: FL: 47 apps 15 gls Total: 47 apps 15 gls

KENNEDY, Samuel

Half-back or Centre-forward
6' 0" 12st 2lbs
Born: Platts Common, 1896
Died: Scunthorpe, 9 December 1963
Career: Wombwell. Huddersfield Town August 1920. Burnley May 1921. Denaby United December 1921. Wombwell August 1922. NELSON February 1924, fee £200. Fulham October 1924. Barnsley October 1926. Mexborough Town March 1927. Shirebrook July 1928. Scunthorpe & Lindsey United June 1929. Brigg Town October 1930. Broughton Rangers September 1931.
Debut v South Shields (h) 2.2.24, lost 0–2

Despite association with five different Football League clubs, Sam Kennedy made only 21 senior appearances and scored six goals. Five of the goals coming from just nine matches for Barnsley, his last League club. A well-known sprinter before becoming a professional footballer, he had yet to feature in League football when he joined Nelson in the late stages of the 1923-24 relegation season. Within his half dozen appearances he occupied three different positions, centre-half, centre-forward and right-half, but failed to shine in any of them. Despite his dashing approach, he lacked ball control and steadiness when in sight of goal. Sam settled in Scunthorpe, working in a local hotel, and in the 1950s he became a director of Scunthorpe United.
Appearances: FL: 6 apps 0 gls Total: 6 apps 0 gls

LAMMUS, William Christmas James

Right-back 5' 11" 12st 0lbs
Born: Barking, 14 August 1898
Died: Southend, January quarter 1982
Career: Barking Town. West Bromwich Albion May 1922. NELSON July 1923. Nuneaton Town July 1924. Tunbridge Wells Rangers. New Beckton Baptists (West Ham) amateur August 1932.
Debut v Stockport County (a) 27.8.23, lost 0–1

As one correspondent put it: "Lammus was inclined to overdo the vigorous. He was a powerful defender for all that, but with a little more judgment he would be of great value." The strapping full-back had not graduated to senior level with West Bromwich Albion, and he did not appear in Nelson's Second Division side beyond an early-season run of eight matches, only one of which was won.
Appearances: FL: 8 apps 0 gls Total: 8 apps 0 gls

LAYCOCK, Frederick Walter

Inside-forward
5' 9"   11st 7lbs
Born: Sheffield, 31 March 1897
Died: Sheffield, 19 September 1989
Career: St Mary's, (Sheffield). Shirebrook cs 1921. Rotherham Town cs 1922. Sheffield Wednesday March 1923. Barrow July 1924, NELSON March 1925, fee £70. Mansfield Town August 1926. New Brighton July 1927, fee £150. Peterborough & Fletton United September 1928. Darlington September 1929. York City June 1930. Swindon Town May 1931. Derry City July 1933. Witton Albion October 1934. Nuneaton Town October 1935. Cannock Town cs 1936. Northwich Victoria (trial) November 1936. Shrewsbury Town (trial) December 1936. Hereford United January 1937.
Debut v Hartlepools United (h) 21.3.25, won 2–0
A player of the 'move every year' fraternity, Fred Laycock was a dangerous forward, outstanding in headwork, who scored a career total of 64 goals in 160 League matches. His transfer to Nelson became the subject of an inquiry, after which both player and club were fined. This was on account of his signing transfer forms while he was actually involved in a match. This most unusual event occurred on the last day for transfers in March 1925, when he was playing for Barrow on Rotherham County's ground. More than one club with representatives at the ground sought his signature. In the event, he was called from the pitch to sign forms, thus finding himself in the curious, and illegal, position of playing for Barrow whilst a Nelson player. His seven goals in 12 matches was an excellent start to his Seedhill career but it was not sufficient to enable Nelson to overtake Darlington at the top of the table, the Quakers taking the championship with Nelson in second place. Despite scoring five goals in 11 League matches in the following season, Laycock was mainly fielded in the reserve team, his contribution of 18 goals helping them to win the championship of the Lancashire Combination for the first time. The reserves were also runners-up for the Combination Cup.
Appearances: FL: 23 apps 12 gls Total: 23 apps 12 gls

LILLEY, Robert 'Bob'

Right-back
5' 7"   11st 7lbs
Born: Bolton, 3 April 1893
Died: Bolton, 12 January 1964
Career: Bridge Street Wesleyans. Bolton West End. Bolton North End. Little Lever Lads. Rochdale August 1914. Royal Field Artillery WW1. Horwich FC 1919-20. NELSON November 1920, registered for FL matches August 1921 to May 1925.
Debut v Wigan Borough (h) 27.8.21, lost 1–2
Bob Lilley joined Nelson prior to Football League entry and quickly earned a reputation as one of the most consistent full-backs in the Central League. He had the misfortune to break his nose in the final match of season 1920-21 at Blackburn Rovers and endured a very bad time, spending some time in hospital before being thoroughly recovered. He was immediately at home in senior football, being fearless in the tackle, very sure in his clearances and quick to recover when passed. He was unfortunate to be very seriously injured for a second time at Tranmere Rovers in October, after just ten matches of the 1922-23 championship campaign and was unable to resume until April 1924, playing in the last five Second Division matches. In his final season, he returned to first team football following the transfer of the former Barrow right-back, Phizacklea, to Preston North End. Summer months were spent behind the stumps as wicket keeper with Heaton in the Lancashire League
Appearances: FL: 66 apps 0 gls FAC: 3 apps 0 gls
Total: 69 apps 0 gls

LILLEY, Thomas

Right-back
5' 11½"   12st 4lbs
Born: New Herrington, January quarter 1900
Died: New Herrington, July quarter 1967
Career: Methley Perseverance. Huddersfield Town November 1922. NELSON November 1923, fee £100. Hartlepools United August 1924. Sunderland May 1926, fee £750. St Mirren August 1928, fee £350. Fulham July 1930, fee £250. Annfield Plain August 1931. New Herrington Welfare February 1932. Shiney Row Swifts. Sunderland District Omnibus, reinstated amateur November 1933. Herrington Colliery Committee February 1955.
Debut v Coventry City (a) 10.11.23, lost 0–4

A tall and powerfully built full-back, Tom Lilley was a man of many clubs who began with Huddersfield Town, making the first of his three appearances at Birmingham on Christmas Day 1922. Nelson's Second Division relegation season was at its mid point before Tom Lilley enjoyed a run of first team matches, and this was terminated when his namesake, Bob Lilley, was recovered from injury and regained his right fullback spot. Two seasons with Hartlepools United brought regular first team football for the first time despite a most unfortunate start in which he twice suffered a broken collar-bone. Ever-present in the following term he attracted the scouts, Sunderland paying a useful fee to take him to Roker Park. Aside from one League outing, his time was spent in reserve, but he found more success in Scottish football, appearing in 62 topflight matches and reaching the semi-final and quarter-final of the Scottish Cup. A move to Fulham completed his senior career and his seven League appearances meant that he had played in all four Divisions of the Football League.

Appearances: FL: 14 apps 0 gls Total: 14 apps 0 gls

McCLURE, David

Right-back   5'10 ½"   12st 6lbs
Born: Slammanan, Stirlingshire
Career: Glenavon. New Brighton (trial) November-December 1923. Dunipace Juniors. St Johnstone October 1924. NELSON June 1927. Dundee United July 1928. Portadown July 1930. Glentoran February 1933. Montrose.
Debut v Durham City (h) 25.9.27, won 2-1

With a fair amount of senior experience in Scottish football, both before and after his season at Seedhill, the ideally built defender emerged as one of the few successes in a Nelson side that sought re-election for the first time in 1927-28. A subsequent spell in Irish soccer saw McClure twice honoured by the Irish League in matches against the Football League at Windsor Park, Belfast, on 1st October 1932, and against the Scottish League at Ibrox Park, Glasgow, on 19th October 1932.

Appearances: FL: 28 apps 1 gl Total: 28 apps 1 gl

McCULLOCH, Michael

Inside-left, later wing-half
5' 8"   10st 10lbs
Born: Denny, Lanarkshire, 26 April 1891
Died: St Andrew, Edinburgh, 21 August 1973
Career: Denny Hibernians. Falkirk July 1913. Heart of Midlothian May 1921. NELSON June 1922, fee £150. Chesterfield June 1924. Bournemouth & Boscombe Athletic March 1925. St Bernard's June 1925.
Debut v Bradford Park Avenue (a) 26.8.22, lost 2-6

Former Scottish Junior International Mick McCulloch captained Falkirk in a lengthy spell at Brockville, clocking up in excess of 160 first team appearances. He joined Nelson after a season with Hearts, and captained his new team to the championship of the Third Division North in his first season. A cool, calculating player who specialised in the close passing game so often associated with ball playing Scots, he was not a big scorer on his own account, his value being in his constructive play and the making of openings for his colleagues. He scored Nelson's first goal in Second Division football, but was then switched from inside-forward to wing-half and played little in the second half of the season. His omission from the side brought a number of letters to the editor of the 'Nelson Leader'. Two typical examples were signed "A lover of Justice" and "Disgusted" and both basically let rip at the directors of the Nelson club for what was perceived as unfair treatment of McCulloch, described by obvious admirers as: "A natural footballer, who has endeared himself to the Nelson followers by reason of his splendid and enthusiastic play on the field and his wholehearted club spirit." Apparently, the said directors were of the opinion that McCulloch didn't play as well in away matches as he did at home. With the club fighting for its very existence in Division Two it did seem, in hindsight, that a player with McCulloch's unquestionable ability was wasted in the reserves.

Appearances: FL: 49 apps 8 gls FAC: 4 apps 0 gls Total: 53 apps 8 gls
Honours: NELSON, Division Three North champions 1923.

McDONAGH, Patrick

Inside-right   5' 9½"   11st 9lbs
Born: Partick, Glasgow, 5 November 1906
Career: St Anthony's. Barnsley August 1926. NELSON June 1928. Bangor City December 1928. Clydebank. Beith July 1933. Brechin City 1934. Workington (trial) cs 1935. Sligo Rovers, to December 1935.
Debut v Southport (a) 8.9.28, lost 1–5

Pat McDonagh failed to capitalise on his bright start in League football. After a lengthy wait for his chance in Division Two with Barnsley, he scored twice on his debut in a 4–2 win against Clapton Orient at Oakwell on 24th September 1927, but in a further eight outings he failed to find the net. His final first team appearance came in early December, and although Barnsley sold their two star forwards, Brook and Tilson, to Manchester City for a joint fee of £6,000 in March, McDonagh was not recalled to League action. Signed by Nelson in the close season, he was released in mid term after new signing James Buchanan immediately impressed at inside-right, embarking on a run of 53 consecutive League appearances.

Appearances: FL: 5 apps 0 gls Total: 5 apps 0 gls

McGREEVY, William James

Inside-right
Born: Fleetwood, 11 November 1899
Died: Fleetwood, January quarter 1981
Career: Fleetwood Athletic. Fleetwood FC amateur August 1921. NELSON amateur April 1922.
Debut v Barrow (h) 17.4.22, drawn 1–1 (scored)

McGreevy's first season with Fleetwood Athletic was success all the way. In 1919-20 they were champions of the Blackpool and District Amateur Football League. Additionally, they won the Blackwell Charity Cup, the Rawlings Challenge Shield and the Fleetwood Football Club Cup and Medals Competition. Their outstanding record for the season was: Played 30, won 27, lost 0, drawn 3, goals for 98, against 12. His elevation to Lancashire Combination level with Fleetwood followed in August 1921, and in the same season he made his Football League debut as an amateur with Nelson, appearing in three late season fixtures, and having the satisfaction of scoring on his debut against Barrow.

Appearances: FL: 3 apps 1 gl Total: 3 apps 1 gl

McGUIRE, John

Centre or Inside-forward
5' 10"   11st 8lbs
Born: Darlington, October quarter 1900
Career: Darlington Railway Athletic. Cockfield. Charlton Athletic August 1925. Wigan Borough November 1926. NELSON December 1927. Darlington July 1928 to cs 1930.
Debut v Ashington (h) 3.12.27, lost 1–5

John McGuire's career spanned exactly 100 League matches and 23 goals, his best spells coming with Wigan Borough (33 matches, 14 goals) and Darlington (42 matches, seven goals). He made his League debut with Charlton Athletic in September 1925, in a disappointing season when they had to seek re-election for the first time. His spell with Nelson was similarly unrewarding, despite his first goal, in his second appearance, being scored against his former team-mates at Wigan Borough's Springfield Park.

Appearances: FL: 20 apps 2 gls Total: 20 apps 2 gls

McKINNELL, James Templeton Broadfoot

Left-half
5' 9"   11st 3lbs
Born: Dalbeattie, Kirkcudbright, 27 March 1893
Died: Brixworth, Northants, October quarter 1972
Career: Dalbeattie Star. Ayr United 1913-14. Nithsdale Wanderers July 1914. Dumfries. Queen of the South Wanderers 1919. Blackburn Rovers December 1920. Darlington July 1926, fee £300. NELSON July 1929 to June 1930. Northampton Town assistant trainer August 1934. Queen of the South manager July 1938 (And still there in January 1947).
Debut v Tranmere Rovers (a) 16.11.29, won 3–2

Jimmy McKinnell was an extremely able wing-half, sound in the tackle and in constructive moves. He actually crossed the border to join

Blackburn Rovers as an inside-forward, but was said to lack pace, and it was not until he was switched to wing-half in late season 1921-22 that his true position was found. After 124 League and Cup appearances for the Rovers he joined Darlington and in three seasons made 109 League and Cup appearances. He also scored what proved to be the only League goal of his career in an 8–2 win against South Shields on 23rd April 1927. Losing out to David Suttie, another former Blackburn Rovers player, for the left-half berth, McKinnell spent much of his Seedhill season in the reserve team. Outside of the game, he worked as a tester at the Arrol Johnson Motor Company, and as a painter and decorator in Northampton.
Appearances: FL: 10 Apps 0 gls FAC: 1 app 0 gls Total: 11 apps 0 gls

McLAUGHLAN, George

Inside-left   5' 8 ½"   11st 2lbs
Career: John Street Secondary School, (Bridgeton). Greenhead Thistle Juniors. Celtic April 1923. Clydebank loan October 1923. Stenhousemuir loan February 1924. Clydebank March 1924. Mid-Rhondda December 1924. Clyde 1925. Darlington 1926. Hull City June 1926. Accrington Stanley May 1927. NELSON June 1929 to May 1930. Morecambe October 1931.
Debut v Southport (h) 31.8.29, drawn 2–2
It seems most likely that Nelson's directors would have taken note of George McLaughlan's stunning debut for Accrington Stanley at Seedhill on the opening Saturday of season 1927-28. He was on the score sheet within 20 minutes of the kick-off and added a second in Stanley's emphatic 4–1 victory. Once described as a "tricky and clever inside-forward", his trickiness was always purposeful and, on moving to Seedhill, he formed a fine left wing partnership with Foster Hedley. In earlier days, McLaughlan played only once for Celtic, in a 1–2 home defeat by Partick Thistle in September 1923, but before crossing the border he won a Glasgow Cup medal with Clyde against Celtic in October 1925. His best spell in English football came in two seasons with Accrington Stanley, for whom he scored 21 goals in 76 League matches. His senior career ended after his season with Nelson, when he was one of eight players given free transfers by the Seedhill management in the close season of 1930.
Appearances: FL: 29 apps 2 gls FAC: 1 app 0 gls Total: 30 apps 2 gls

MACE, Fred

Goalkeeper   6' 0"   12st 5lbs
Born: Hayfield, October quarter 1895
Died: Wooley, Cheshire, 5 November 1962, age 66
Career: Godley Athletic. Copley Celtic. Stalybridge Celtic 1919. NELSON May 1925, fee £100. Macclesfield Town August 1927.
Debut v Chesterfield (h) 20.4.26, drawn 3–3
In a lengthy association with Stalybridge Celtic, Fred Mace was regarded as one of the best goalkeepers operating in the Cheshire League. Throughout his two years at Seedhill, Mace was unable to dislodge Harry Abbott, but he gave excellent service in the Lancashire Combination side. Missing only one match in his first season, he materially contributed to the success of the team in winning the championship of the Lancashire Combination. He was one of ten Nelson players placed on the transfer list in May 1927, in his case the listing came after he had refused terms for the following season.
Appearances: FL: 8 apps 0 gls Total: 8 apps 0 gls

MANGHAM, James

Goalkeeper   5' 10"   11st 0lbs
Born: Cliviger, 1 March 1907
Died: Burnley, 23 October 1995
Career: Worsthorne. Portsmouth Rovers September 1924. NELSON amateur August 1927 to November 1929.
Debut v Hartlepools United (a) 17.3.28, won 5–4
Nelson were extremely poor travellers in season 1927-28 and their visit to Hartlepools did not appear to offer any grounds for optimism. Their form, however, was a revelation and the 5–4 victory might have been even more convincing, for 21 year-old amateur goalkeeper Mangham, deputising for Warhurst, obviously lacked experience and confidence. He should not have beaten as often as he was, although one of Hartlepools' goals was an unfortunate own goal by Clem Rigg. The local 'keeper had a lengthy wait for a second opportunity and when it came he was on the receiving end of a six-goal blast by Darlington in the second fixture of 1929-30. His amateur registration was cancelled in November of the same season, as the club had three other professional goalkeepers on their books, and only two teams to play them in.
Appearances: FL: 2 apps 0 gls Total: 2 apps 0 gls

MANOCK, Edward

Inside-right   5' 9"   11st 5lbs
Born: Salford, 30 June 1904
Died: Blyth, Notts, 12 April 1983
Career: Chester amateur. NELSON amateur November1929, professional January 1930 to May 1931. Sandbach Ramblers. Pendleton Glass Works amateur October 1934. CWS Glass Works (Worksop) amateur September 1936.
Debut v Southport (a) 28.12.29, drawn 0–0

53

In Nelson's final two seasons of League football the team was reshuffled, almost from week to week, as the directors strove to find a combination capable of halting the slide into oblivion. With the odd exception, it was clear that the playing staff was just not up to the standard required for Third Division football. Rather ironically, however, in one of Ted Manock's infrequent first team appearances at Doncaster Rovers in October 1930, when he was fielded out of position on the right wing, Nelson went down by 2–0. Back at Seedhill, on the same afternoon, the reserves beat Accrington Stanley Reserves 10–3, prompting another major reshuffle of the first team for the following week's trip to Crewe Alexandra. Little improvement was made, however, as the side with seven changes lost 2–4, the eighth defeat within the space of the opening eleven matches.

Appearances: FL: 18 apps 2 gls Total: 18 apps 2 gls

MARSH, Cecil William B.

Forward or Half-back
5' 8 ½"   11st 3lbs
Born: Darnall, Sheffield, October quarter 1890
Died: Blackpool, July quarter 1956, aged 65
Career: Beighton Recreation. Sheffield United February 1916. Craven Sports 1918. Blackpool May 1919. NELSON April 1921. Fleetwood player-coach October 1922.
Debut v Wigan Borough (h) 27.8.21, lost 1–2

Cecil Marsh was severely wounded in World War One but made a full recovery and was able to commence with Blackpool when normal League football resumed in season 1919-20. A speedy and resourceful forward, who could also play at half-back, he was a regular in the Seasiders' Central League side for two seasons, with a record of 43 goals scored and selection for the Central League team who beat the North Eastern League side by 2–0 at St James' Park, Newcastle, on 22nd January 1921. Some three months later he joined Nelson who were in the final weeks of their last campaign in the Central League. He commenced in League football with Nelson at right-half, was quickly switched to inside-right, and before losing his place in mid season, occupied both extreme wing positions.

Appearances: FL: 17 apps 2 gls FAC: 2 apps 0 gls
Total: 19 apps 2 gls

MARTIN, John Charles

Centre-half
6' 0"   13st 6lbs
Born: North Leeds, 25 July 1903
Died: Padiham, 31 December 1976
Career: Hale Hill Wesleyan School. Barnoldswick Park Villa. Padiham. Burnley 'A' Team January 1923. Accrington Stanley amateur July, professional November 1924. Blackpool February 1926, fee £1,350. Southport June 1927. Macclesfield Town July 1929. Southport May 1930 NELSON November 1930, fee £200. Wigan Borough July 1931. Oldham Athletic November 1931 to May 1932, fee £50.
Debut v Carlisle United (a) 8.11.30, lost 1–2

A hefty centre-half who gave the ball plenty of boot out of defence, Jack Martin's early promise as a 'stopper' centre-half earned Accrington Stanley a sizeable fee, but his stay with Blackpool was not a success, failure to develop the constructive side of his game resulting in his time at Bloomfield Road being spent at reserve level. Without ever leaving Lancashire, he assisted seven League clubs. He must have thought himself jinxed when he endured successive hammer blows with both Nelson and Wigan Borough, both clubs losing their Football League status while he was on their books. His final move, to Oldham Athletic, was ended by a knee injury that enforced his retirement. He subsequently became a coal merchant in Padiham and then worked as a tackler in the weaving industry.

Appearances: FL: 27 apps 1 gl FAC: 3 apps 0 gls
Total: 30 apps 1 gl

MELLOR, Harold 'Harry'

Centre-forward   5' 6 ½"   10st 10lbs
Born: Fylde, July quarter 1895
Career: South Shore. NELSON July 1921. South Shore September 1922. Eccles United August 1926. New Mills July 1927.
Debut v Accrington Stanley (h) 15.11.21, lost 0 - 1

The local correspondent considered that Harry Mellor's debut was "A trying ordeal". Introduced as a late replacement for the Irish international Halligan, who had suffered a back strain in training, Mellor, without experience in senior football, did not impress. Offered minimal support by his more experienced inside forward colleagues, the whole front line disappointed in

the 1–0 defeat by Lancashire rivals Accrington Stanley, who brought with them an estimated 3,000 spectators, boosting the attendance to between 13,000 and 14,000. The receipts, incidentally, amounted to a little over £560 - £200 more than the previous record for the Seedhill enclosure.
Appearances: FL: 1 app 0 gls Total: 1 app 0 gls

METCALFE, James Alfred

Right-half
5' 8 ½"   11st 4lbs
Born: Whitburn, Sunderland, 10 December 1898
Died: Preston, 20 February 1975
Career: Sunderland Schoolboys. Sunderland Royal Rovers. Southwick. South Shields April 1920. Preston North End June 1927. NELSON June 1928 to May 1930, fee £250. Preston North End trainer July 1931. Leicester City trainer July 1939, and for a second time in August 1949.
Debut v Hartlepools United (a) 25.8.28, drawn 2–2
James Metcalfe began with Sunderland Boys, winning his first medal in the Children's Hospital Cup competition. Before entering League football with South Shields he won several awards with Southwick including the Ship-owners' Cup medal, the Eye Infirmary medal and a runners-up award in the Monkwearmouth Charity Cup. In a seven-year association with South Shields, the remarkably durable and consistent wing-half clocked up 185 Second Division appearances, 99 of which were made consecutively. A season with Preston North End followed, and he cost Nelson a tidy sum in the summer of 1928. Constructive and stylish, he worked hard defensively and in backing-up his attack. After retiring as a player he spent lengthy spells on the training staff of Preston North End and Leicester City. Both during after leaving the game he spent most Sundays performing as a church organist.
Appearances: FL: 71 apps 1 gl Total: 71 apps 1 gl

MITCHELL, Ronald

Left-half
5' 9 ½"   12st 0lbs
Born: Birkenhead, July quarter 1902
Career: Dick, Kerr's. Skelmersdale United amateur. Liverpool June 1922, fee £75. Hull City May 1924. NELSON May 1926, fee £50. Bristol Rovers June 1927. Mossley July 1928. Great Harwood July 1929. Fleetwood Windsor Villa December 1929.
Debut v Wigan Borough (a) 28.8.26, lost 1- 2
Billed as "An adaptable and clever player" on signing from Hull City, Mitchell slotted well into Nelson's middle line, alongside captain George Wilson and the vastly experienced Jim Baker. Stronger in defence than attack, he enjoyed a good season at Seedhill, assisting the side to finish fifth in the Northern Section. At the outset of his career he spent two seasons with Liverpool without reaching senior level. In two seasons with Hull City he made 27 League appearances and scored one goal. After leaving Nelson, he did not feature in Bristol Rovers' first team.
Appearances: FL: 32 apps 0 gls FAC: 2 apps 0 gls Total: 34 apps 0 gls

MOORE, Walter

Outside-right, later Right-back
5' 6"   10st 10lbs
Born: Darfield, near Barnsley, January quarter 1899
Career: West Melton Excelsior. Darfield. NELSON March 1924. Wath Athletic cs 1925 to 1927. Winterwell Athletic September 1932.
Debut v Halifax Town (h) 25.10.24, won 2–1
Although signed as an outside-right, the diminutive Walter Moore shone most brightly as an emergency full-back in the late stages of season 1924-25. His display in the 2–1 victory against Southport at Seedhill on 21st April certainly impressed the local correspondent: "Moore's display at full-back was a revelation, for where he failed in height he made up in courage and speed. His whole hearted display was thoroughly to the liking of the spectators." Two incidents from the match concerned his tussles with Southport's winger, the much taller Fergie Aitken: "The crowd was roused to much amusement by two sprints between the diminutive Moore and F. Aitken and as they

ended in favour of the Nelsonian the crowd was raised to enthusiasm."
Appearances: FL: 5 apps 0 gls Total: 5 apps 0 gls

MORTON, William

Centre-forward
Born: Most probably in Northumberland
Career: Bedlington P.M. Newbiggin West End. Durham City 1927. Craghead United. NELSON amateur January, professional February 1929 Craghead United August 1929. Bedlington United February 1930. Blyth Spartans September 1930. Queens Park Rangers November 1930. Craghead United January 1931. Ashington August 1932. Stakeford Albion June 1933.
Debut v Stockport County (h) 22.1.29, won 4–1 (scored two)

A typical contemporary press comment on the centre-forward's abilities was: "Morton worked energetically, but was on the slow side". This verdict giving some inkling as to his lack of first team opportunities, despite a most encouraging two-goal debut against Stockport County. Mainly as understudy to Bernard Radford, the team's most successful marksman with 24 goals in 35 matches, Morton was largely employed in the reserve team. This was also his level with both Durham City and Queens Park Rangers.
Appearances: FL: 8 apps 3 gls Total: 8 apps 3 gls

NEWNES, John 'Jack'

Half-back
5' 9½"   11st 6lbs
Born: Trefnant, St Asaph, Denbighshire, 6 June 1895
Died: Salford, 3 February 1969
Career: Whitchurch. Brymbo Institute 1919-22. Bolton Wanderers May 1922. NELSON September 1923. Southport October 1926. Mossley July 1928. Manchester North End February 1930. Winsford United 1931-32. Glossop August 1932. Altrincham cs 1933. Manchester North End player-coach September 1935.
Debut v Southampton (h) 11.9.23, drawn 0–0

Jack Newnes' standing in the history of Nelson FC is quite without equal, as he was the only player to be capped at international level whilst on the Seedhill playing register. His big day came on 13th February 1926, when he represented Wales against Northern Ireland in Belfast. Sadly, however, there was no fairytale ending as the Irish won 3–0. A former steel worker and collier, he was a late starter in League football when he joined Bolton Wanderers when a month short of his 27th birthday. He made his debut in the First Division, in a 4–2 win against Nottingham Forest on 2nd January 1923 and totalled seven League appearances. He did not appear in the season's run in the FA Cup that took Bolton to the first Wembley Final, and a 2–0 victory against West Ham United. He was secured by Nelson in the early weeks of the following season for an undisclosed but record fee for the club, and in a three-year stay proved to be a sound investment. A neat player who went about his work unobtrusively, he excelled in constructive play from either centre or right-half, and was a reliable taker of penalty kicks, netting his first in Nelson's initial win in Second Division football against Stoke in September 1923. Southport was his final port of call in League football, but his non-League career continued beyond his 40th year. Jack Newnes served during World War One with the Royal Welch Fusiliers, and in later years worked as salesman in the Manchester fruit and vegetable market.
Appearances: FL: 113 apps 7 gls FAC: 5 apps 0 gls Total: 118 apps 7 gls
Honours: Wales International, 1 cap 1926

NUTTALL, Robert

Wing-half or Centre-forward
5' 9"   11st 5lbs
Born: Tottington, 1 May 1908
Died: Ramsbottom, 10 January 1983
Career: Tottington FC. NELSON amateur February 1930. Turton FC November 1933. Tottington St John's amateur October 1935.
Debut v York City (a) 21.3.31, lost 2–5

Arriving at Seedhill in the final weeks of League football, all four of Nuttall's senior appearances ended in heavy defeats as the team slid into the abyss, having taken only 19 points from 42 League matches. The versatile youngster remained at Seedhill for the following season when Nelson re-commenced in non-League circles, with the 'Nelson Leader' imploring the public to support the town's club, noting "Reduced prices of admission now 6d. Stands and Enclosures extra".
Appearances: FL: 4 apps 0 gls Total: 4 apps 0 gls

NUTTER, Henry "Harry"

Goalkeeper
Born: Nelson circa 1901
Career: Barnoldswick Town. NELSON amateur February 1924.
Debut v South Shields (a) 9.2.24, lost 0–2

Amateur Harry Nutter was recruited at a time when first team goalkeeper Abbott was experiencing injury problems. In addition to playing football, Nutter was also a keen runner who lived locally at 14 Vernon Street and his working life centred around the local textile industry at both Mather Brothers, Hapton, and James Tattersall & Sons, Seed Hill Mills, Nelson. Originally scheduled for a trial in the reserves, he was first pressed into action for senior duty at South Shields. Only three players retained their positions from the previous week as the directors wielded the axe in what proved to be an unsuccessful effort to halt a depressing run of results. South Shields' victory by three goals to nil flattered them, as Nelson held their own until quarter of an hour from full-time but then conceded three goals in rapid succession. The third goal came from the penalty spot after Nutter went out to fist the ball and in the process was alleged to have connected with the chin of a South Shields forward! Both Nelson's, and Nutter's, experiences in Second Division football continued unhappily with the visit of Bury, one week later. As the local correspondent observed: "Nelson were like the man who fell out of the balloon – they were not in it." Whacked by five goals to none, the defence was over-run, Nutter was said to have done many smart things in goal, but his inexperience proved costly, as he was not blameless for two of Bury's goals. In October 1925 he joined the Lancashire Constabulary, but left the force in the following year, and on November 5th was one of 931 passengers who embarked from Liverpool on the S.S. Demosthenes, bound for Melbourne, Australia. At the time of sailing, his occupation was listed as Cellar Man. Some twenty years later, the Nelson Football Club were pleased to hear from their former player when they received a donation of £10 from him, for club funds. At that time Harry Nutter was living at Kew, Victoria. He is thought to have died in Victoria, Australia in 1983.

Appearances: FL: 2 apps 0 gls Total: 2 apps 0 gls

O'BEIRNE, Patrick Joseph

Inside-left
5' 9"   11st 7lbs
Born: Waterford, 15 June 1900
Died: Manchester, July quarter 1980
Career: Army football (Welch Regiment). Norman Athletic 1920. Stalybridge Celtic amateur May 1921, professional March 1922. Burnley August 1923. NELSON June 1924, fee £150. Middlewich (loan) December 1925. Congleton Town cs 1928. Manchester Central June 1930. Stalybridge Celtic November 1931.
Debut v Southport (a) 30.8.24, lost 0–1

Joe O'Beirne was born in Waterford and moved to Manchester with his parents when young. He made his League debut with Stalybridge Celtic, playing in just one match in the first season of the Third Division North (1921-22) and in nine matches in 1922-23. A season with Burnley followed, but as understudy to Benny Cross for the inside-left berth he was restricted to just five First Division appearances. Beginning as first choice on arrival at Seedhill, he lost out in mid season when Edgar Chadwick was preferred at inside-left. Outside of the game he was employed as a compositor in the printing industry.

Appearances: FL: 16 apps 2 gls FAC: 2 apps 1 gl
Total: 18 apps 3 gls

PARRY, Frank Thomas

Outside-right
5' 7"   11st 2lbs
Born: Aigburth, Liverpool, 14 June 1898
Died: Southport, 13 March 1973
Career: Everton November 1921, Grimsby Town June 1926. Accrington Stanley July 1927. NELSON November 1929 to May 1930. Felling Stanley September 1930.
Debut v Lincoln City (h) 9.11.27,

57

drawn 0–0

Born into a footballing family, Frank's father was Maurice Price Parry, a prominent wing-half with Liverpool and Wales in the early 1900s. An uncle, Tom D. Parry, played for Oswestry and Wales in the same period. Frank Parry began with Everton and was mainly a reserve team player throughout, Sam Chedgzoy dominating the outside-right position. He arrived at Accrington Stanley from Grimsby Town with only 13 League outings to his name, but in a little over two seasons at Peel Park he made 81 League appearances and scored 10 goals. A skilful and polished winger, his only flaw was said to be a lack of confidence in his own ability as a goal scorer. He missed only four matches during his spell with Nelson, revealing clever touches and an ability to occupy both wings with equal faculty.
Appearances: FL: 24 apps 2 gls FAC: 1 app 0 gls
Total: 25 apps 2 gls

PEARSON, James Stevens

Full-back 5' 8"   11st 0lbs
Born: Heywood, January quarter 1905
Died: Blackpool, 24 January 1962
Career: Heywood. NELSON amateur April, professional September 1925. Hurst June 1928. Newark Town September 1929. Runcorn September 1932.
Debut v Coventry City (a) 3.10.25, lost 0–1
As deputy for defensive stalwart Clem Rigg at left full-back, Pearson made his senior debut at Coventry City, lining up behind his cousin, Ernie Braidwood who occupied the left-half role. The youthful defender spent most of his first full season in the reserves who won the Lancashire Combination championship for the first time, winning 27 of their 38 league engagements and scoring 123 goals. The team endured only one disappointment, failing to achieve a 'double' when beaten by Fleetwood in the Combination Cup Final. Pearson appeared in most matches, partnering Walter Chadwick at full-back. In the following season he enjoyed lengthy spells of first team football when the team were strong contenders for promotion up to Easter, but then failed to gain a single point from the last six matches and finished fifth in the table. His final season was Nelson's worst, they conceded 136 goals – a record for the Third Division and, not surprisingly, they finished at the foot of the table and had to seek re-admission to the League. Only six players were re-engaged, Pearson stepping down into non-League circles, initially with Hurst of the Cheshire League.
Appearances: FL: 38 apps 0 gls FAC: 2 apps 0 gls
Total: 40 apps 0 gls

PHIZACKLEA, James Robert

Left-back
5'10 ½"   11st 9lbs
Born: Barrow-in-Furness, 29 September 1898
Died: Ardleigh, Essex, 28 May 1971
Career: Barrow Hindpool Athletic. Barrow Submarine Engine Athletic. Barrow June 1921. NELSON June 1924. Preston North End January 1925, fee £1,000. South Shields July 1926. Thames Association August 1928. Stockport County August 1930. Guildford City. Roneo Sports, Romford, amateur October 1931.
Debut v Southport (a) 30.8.24, lost 0–1
A cool and thoughtful defender whose outstanding form in the first half of season 1924-25 earned him an upward move to Preston North End, netting a very welcome fee, for a player who had cost Nelson nothing some seven months earlier. In three seasons with Barrow he completed 76 League and Cup appearances and scored three goals. Said to have revealed "Sterling qualities" on his arrival at Deepdale, he was nevertheless unable to prevent North End's relegation from the top flight. A change of manager found Phizacklea out of favour, leading to his eventual transfer to South Shields. In two seasons at Horsley Hill he completed 68 League appearances, but he did not feature at senior level again with either Thames or Stockport County. Family details from the 1901 Census revealed that James was the son of John – a riveter's holder-up – and mother Sarah, a beer-house keeper. Their accommodation must have been stretched to the very limit, as it housed a further five children, two nephews and four boarders.
Appearances: FL: 19 apps 0 gls FAC: 2 apps 0 gls
Total: 21 apps 0 gls

PICKERING, Thomas

Centre-forward
Born: Egremont, Cumberland, October quarter 1906
Career: Egremont. NELSON amateur 1st January, professional 6th January 1927. Egremont March 1927. Parton Athletic August 1927.
Debut v Wrexham (h) 1.1.27, won 3–0
An injury sustained by Jimmy Hampson at Wrexham on 27th December 1926 proved to be more serious than anticipated, and he was unable

to play in the return fixture on New Year's Day 1927. Nelson's directors made the bold experiment of playing amateur leader Tom Pickering, of Egremont, but although Nelson's home record was maintained, Pickering did not impress in what proved to be a solitary outing at senior level.
Appearances: FL: 1 app 0 gls Total: 1 app 0 gls

PRICE, James

Centre-half
5' 10½"   12st 2lbs
Born: Annbank, 24 April 1896
Career: Cumnock Juniors. Celtic August 1918. Dumbarton loan January 1919. Airdreonians June 1921. NELSON January 1922. Ashington March 1923. North Shields May 1930. Ashington December 1930. Wallaw United player and trainer. Ashington trainer August 1933.
Debut v Wrexham (h) 2.1.22, won 4–0

The Ayrshire village of Annbank produced any number of footballers who reached professional level in both the Scottish and English game, and Jimmy Price was a typical example. The former Celtic pivot took over from Jacques in Nelson's middle line and immediately brought about an improvement in the team's defensive capabilities. A tireless worker whose headwork was a feature of his play, he also tackled well and used the ball constructively. After leaving Seedhill, he served Ashington with great distinction, amassing 232 League appearances for the Portland Park club before continuing as trainer when his playing career ended.
Appearances: FL: 24 apps 0 gls Total: 24 apps 0 gls

PROCTOR, Wilfred

Outside-left   5' 8"   11st 0lbs
Born: Fenton, Stoke-on-Trent, 23 November 1893
Died: Blackpool, 29 October 1980
Career: South Shore. Blackpool 1920. NELSON May 1921. Fleetwood August 1922. Lancaster Town July 1925.
Debut v Wigan Borough (h) 27.8.21, lost 1–2

Apparently rejoicing in the nickname 'Wyn', Proctor was without League experience when he joined Nelson for their first season in the Football League, and his debut was made in the season's opener against Wigan Borough. Despite a goal by Bill Halligan after just two minutes play, Wigan spoilt the party by winning 2–1. Proctor held on to the outside-left spot during the next ten matches, of which only two were lost. Thereafter, the team's form took a nosedive and Proctor lost out to a combined challenge from Cecil Marsh, a former Blackpool team mate, and Jim Wootton, who held the left wing spot for much of the second half of the season.
Appearances: FL: 14 apps 1 gl FAC: 2 apps 0 gls Total: 16 apps 1 gl

RADFORD, Bernard

Centre or Inside-forward
5' 9"   11st 0lbs
Born: West Melton, near Rotherham, 23 January 1908
Died: Basingstoke, 2 October 1986
Career: Dearne Valley O.B. Wath Athletic February 1925. Wombwell May 1926. Darfield August 1927. NELSON December 1927. Sheffield United May 1929, fee £850. Northampton Town July 1931, fee £350. Royal Navy Depot, Chatham, amateur October 1932. Banstead Mental Hospital amateur December 1934.
Debut v Doncaster Rovers (h) 17.12.27, lost 0–1

After succeeding Nelson's star centre-forward, Jimmy Hampson, in mid season 1927-28, Bernard Radford rose to the challenge by scoring 17 goals in 20 matches, his total including a hat-trick against Rochdale, and four against Wrexham. Noted for his solo dashes and strong shooting, he continued to find the net on a regular basis during 1928-29, scoring 24 goals in 35 matches. He was very much the mainstay of the attack, the next highest scorer, Halliwell, scored just nine goals in 32 matches. Sadly, Nelson were unable to hang on to their prolific attack leader, although the fee received from Sheffield United enabled summer wages to be paid. Radford's career declined after his Seedhill exploits, the step up from Third Division to the top flight with Sheffield United proved a difficult transition. Sparingly used, he netted seven goals in 20 League matches. He subsequently played in only eight matches for Northampton Town before dropping into non-League football.
Appearances: FL: 55 apps 41 gls Total: 55 apps 41 gls

RAISBECK, Leslie

Centre-forward   5' 10"   12st 0lbs
Born: Shotley Bridge, County Durham, 23 May 1907
Died: Consett, 24 August 1990
Career: Benfieldside St Cuthbert's. Willington December 1925. Tow Law Town. Stockport County amateur August, professional October 1927. NELSON July 1930. Stockport County 1931. Stalybridge Celtic April 1932. Buxton September 1932. Northwich Victoria July 1933.
Debut v New Brighton (a) 20.9.30, drawn 2–2
Nelson's schoolteacher centre-forward began in senior football with Stockport County. His League debut was made on New Year's Day 1929, and he opened the scoring in a 2–1 win against Wigan Borough. Aside from one FA Cup appearance in the same season – a 1–0 win against Halifax Town – he did not feature again in the first team. Despite his lack of experience, he was Nelson's best forward in his season at Seedhill, his height and weight proving very useful in the centre and he was not easily shaken off the ball. In a decidedly shot shy attack (43 goals scored in 42 League matches), Raisbeck's 11 goals in 29 matches was a creditable return and his four FA Cup goals included a hat-trick against Workington in round one.
Appearances: FL: 29 apps 11 gls FAC: 3 apps 4 gls Total: 32 apps 15 gls

RICHMOND, Gilbert

Full-back
5' 9½"   12st 0lbs
Born: Bolton, 2 April 1909
Died: Registered at Durham South East, October quarter 1958.
Career: Burnley amateur November 1929. NELSON amateur February, professional March 1930. Clitheroe June 1931. Burnley May 1932 to September 1939. Wartime guest player with Aldershot and Rochdale. Coaching appointment in Sweden in 1947.
Debut v Doncaster Rovers (a) 1.3.30, lost 0–3
When Gilbert Richmond was signed by Nelson, the 'Lancashire Daily Post Annual' introduced him as: "A half-back, with some experience in Bolton district football." He had also had a spell on amateur forms with Burnley, and later in his career he returned to Turf Moor and played in 193 League and Cup matches for the Clarets before the outbreak of the Second World War. A highlight being his appearance in the 1935 FA Cup semi-final against Sheffield Wednesday at Villa Park, Wednesday accounting for Second Division Burnley and going on to lift the trophy by defeating West Bromwich Albion at Wembley. Richmond's association with Nelson came in the late stages of their time as a Football League club and from the outset he was fielded as a full-back. Adaptable on either flank, he was mobile, a hard tackler, and kicked a long ball, rarely indulging in anything ornamental. He was reported to have an artistic flair, however, his hobbies included pencil sketching.
Appearances: FL: 21 apps 0 gls Total: 21 apps 0 gls

RIDGE, Dennis Hazelwood

Half-back
Born: Wortley, Sheffield, 18 March 1904
Died: Leeds, October quarter 1966
Career: Ecclesfield United. Halifax Town amateur March 1927. NELSON August 1927. Scarborough July 1928. Scarborough Electric amateur September 1933. Playing in the Scarborough Junior Imperial League August 1935.
Debut v Ashington (h) 3.12.27, lost 1–5
Shock-haired Dennis Ridge, the son of a blacksmith, played mainly reserve team football during his season at Seedhill. As the League side surrendered 136 goals – a record for the Third Division – he was sparingly used, his best run in the first team being five consecutive matches during the month of April. Released at the end of the season, he joined Scarborough and in his second season at the Athletic Ground appeared in 37 matches in the title winning side who carried off the Midland League championship, scoring 143 goals in the 50-match tournament.
Appearances: FL: 8 apps 0 gls Total: 8 apps 0 gls

RIDLEY, Henry 'Harry'

Outside-left   5' 7½"   11st 0lbs
Born: Sunderland, 25 November 1904
Died: Fulwell, Sunderland, 16 March 1989
Career: Spennymoor United. Fulham (trial) 1926. Spennymoor United. Aldershot. NELSON July 1928. West Stanley August 1929. Workington August 1930. Spennymoor United August 1931. Blyth Spartans July 1933. Murton Colliery Welfare

60

September 1934. Spennymoor United December 1934.
Debut v Hartlepools United (a) 25.8.28, drawn 2–2 (scored one)

Harry Ridley scored in his first and last matches for Nelson. Having netted the opening goal of the new season on his debut, he netted the last in the 4–4 draw at Accrington Stanley that wound up the campaign. The re-constructed side did well to finish in 15th place, only six players being retained from the previous season that ended with a re-election application. Financial difficulties continued to hamper any real progress, however, during the season five players were transferred and in the close season, the club's chief goal scorer, Bernard Radford was transferred to Sheffield United. Only nine professionals were retained at the end of the season and the number did not include Harry Ridley, who returned to non-League football with West Stanley.

Appearances: FL: 31 apps 7 gls Total: 31 apps 7 gls

RIGG, Clement

Left-back
5' 11"   10st 6lbs
Born: Lydgate, Todmorden, 7 February 1899
Died: Todmorden, October quarter 1966
Career: Todmorden Juniors. Portsmouth Rovers. NELSON June 1920, registered for FL matches August 1921. Stalybridge Celtic (trial) September 1929. Newcastle United October 1929.
Debut v Accrington Stanley (a) 8.10.21, lost 1–4

Nelson's record appearance holder Clem Rigg was a worthy successor to Sam Wadsworth, the England international full-back who left Seedhill to join Huddersfield Town just prior to Nelson's election to the Football League. A splendidly consistent left-back who had all the qualities needed: strength in the tackle, coolness under pressure, and the ability to use the ball constructively out of defence. Much sought after by First Division clubs throughout his long association, he was happy to spend his best years at Seedhill, playing regularly until season 1928-29 when he was strongly challenged by the emerging Harry Hooper. Full-backs rarely ventured over the half-way line in the inter war years, and were unlikely to appear on the score sheet. Clem Rigg's four goals all came in season 1924-25 when he took over as the team's penalty kicker with some success. He converted two spot kicks in the 2–0 win against Barrow on 24th January and added another in the next match, a 4–1 victory against Tranmere Rovers.

Appearances: FL: 254 apps 4 gls FAC: 12 apps 0 gls
Total: 266 apps 4 gls
Honours: NELSON: Third Division North champions 1923.

ROBERTS, Percy

Centre-forward   5' 10"   11st 0lbs
Born: Wrexham
Career: Oak Alyn Rovers. Wrexham. Oswestry Town cs 1925. NELSON August 1926. Ashton National (trial) May 1927. Macclesfield Town June 1927. Birmingham City Police amateur March 1928.
Debut v Stoke City (a) 11.9.26, lost 1–4

Although Nelson were the first team to score against Stoke in season 1926-27, it was of little satisfaction as the Potters ran out comfortable winners and eventually won the championship, thereby regaining their Second Division status after just one season in the Third Division North. Nelson's experiment of playing Percy Roberts at centre-forward, in place of the injured Jimmy Hampson, was not a success. He was short of experience, and thought he was reported to have "bustled about to some purpose," the local press reported that "Something else in Third Division football is required beyond that." Ironically, the best man on the field was Stoke's full-back, Billy Spencer, a Nelson native who had first come into prominence while playing in Nelson medal competitions. The former mill worker was a fixture in Stoke's rearguard for over a decade, clocking up 354 League and Cup appearances.

Appearances: FL: 1 app 0 gls Total: 1 app 0 gls

ROBINSON, Ernest Grove S. R.

Right-back
5' 9½"   11st 6lbs
Born: Shiney Row, 21 January 1908
Died: Vancouver, Canada, 1991
Career: Shiney Row Swifts. Houghton Colliery Welfare. Shildon amateur June 1926. York City amateur August 1927, professional August 1928. Notts County May 1929. NELSON June 1930. Northampton Town (trial) March 1931.

61

Tunbridge Wells Rangers July 1931. Barnsley July 1932. Sheffield United May 1933, fee £750. Carlisle United August 1934, fee £175. Lincoln City August 1935 to September 1939. Post-war was trainer-coach to Twente Enschede (Holland).
Debut v Rochdale (a) 30.8.30, lost 4–5

Ernie Robinson made his Football League debut with Nelson. In a struggling side, he held his place for 28 consecutive matches, throughout which he was warmly praised for his whole-hearted approach. In March of the same season he was released when offered a trial with Northampton Town, which unfortunately did not lead to a permanent engagement. He then resumed his career in non-League circles with Tunbridge Wells Rangers. Better things were in store, however, as the former collier eventually played in the First Division with Sheffield United, and a lengthy career was only halted by the outbreak of World War Two. Post war he worked in Holland with Twente Enschede and in 1985, when well beyond retirement age, he emigrated to Canada.

Appearances: FL: 27 apps 0 gls FAC: 3 apps 0 gls
Total: 30 apps 0 gls

ROBINSON, Henry

Outside-left   5' 8½"   11st 0lbs
Born: Chilton, *circa* 1909
Career: Chilton School. Kirk Merrington. Shildon Athletic. Chilton Colliery Railway Athletic cs 1929. Sunderland amateur September, professional October 1929. NELSON May 1930. Hartlepools United February to April 1931. Spennymoor United August 1931. Darlington August 1932. Crook Town September 1932. Horden Colliery Welfare September 1933.
Debut v Rochdale (a) 30.8.30, lost 4–5

The worst season in Nelson's history ended when they lost their Third Division status, being replaced by Chester at the Football League meeting in June 1931. Former Sunderland Reserve wingman Henry Robinson spent much of the first half of the fateful campaign in the first team but was released, mainly for financial reasons, as monetary problems became ever more acute. In a season of unremitting gloom, a glimmer of light came in the FA Cup competition. Accounting for Workington by 4–0 in the first round, round two was reached for the first time since 1926-27. York City drew 1–1 at Seedhill and won the replay 3–2, despite an early goal from Robinson.

Appearances: FL: 20 apps 3 gls FAC: 3 apps 1 gl
Total: 23 apps 4 gls

ROSEBOOM, Edward

Inside-right
5' 8"   11st 7lbs
Born: Govan, 24 November 1896
Died: Kensington, January quarter 1980
Career: Highland Light Infantry. Strathclyde. Fulham (trial) November 1919. Ton Pentre cs 1920. Pontypridd. Cardiff City April 1921. Blackpool December 1921. NELSON August 1923. Clapton Orient February 1924. Rochdale July 1924. Chesterfield July 1925. Mansfield Town June 1929. Newark Town August 1930. Mexborough October 1931.
Debut v Clapton Orient (a) 1.9.23, lost 1–5

One of several new men recruited for Nelson's debut in the Second Division, snappy dresser Ted Roseboom, a former Sergeant Major in the Highland Light Infantry, revealed clever touches, shrewd passing, and the ability to engineer openings for his colleagues. Sadly, in a disappointing season, he was in and out of the side, constant team changes failing to halt the team's slide back into Third Division football. Roseboom departed before the end of the season, and subsequently enjoyed a career spanning 221 League appearances and fifty goals, a large proportion of which (124 matches and 38 goals) was made during his four-year spell with Chesterfield.

Appearances: FL: 12 apps 1 gl FAC: 2 apps 0 gls
Total: 14 apps 1 gl

RUFFELL, William George

Inside-forward   5' 9"   10st 10lbs
Born: Poplar, 29 April 1905
Died: Penzance, March 1988
Career: West Ham United amateur June, professional October 1925. NELSON August 1927. Crewe Alexandra (trial) September 1928. Stockport County (trial) October 1928. Epsom Town.
Debut v Southport (a) 17.9.27, won 2–1

The younger brother of West Ham and England outside-left Jimmy Ruffell who completed 548 appearances and scored 166 goals for the Hammers in a stay of over 18 years. In stark contrast, Bill's only experience in League football was with Nelson, as he did not reach senior level with West Ham United, and subsequently failed to find another League club after unsuccessful trials with both Crewe Alexandra and Stockport County.

Appearances: FL: 12 apps 2 gls Total: 12 apps 2 gls

SANDBACH, Charles

Left-half
Born: Northwich, 8 December 1909
Died: Bury, January 1990
Career: NELSON amateur December 1930. Northampton Town 1931. Northwich Victoria 1933-34.
Debut v Rochdale (a) 27.12.30, drawn 0-0

As deputy for former Blackburn Rovers left-half David Suttie, Charlie Sandbach was called upon just twice in Nelson's final season of League Football. In addition to his debut above, he was on the winning side in his second appearance, a 3-2 victory against Halifax Town at Seedhill. He did not feature in Northampton Town's League side, moving to Northwich Victoria during the 1933-34 season, where he teamed up with another former Nelson player, Leslie Raisbeck. The 'Vics' had a poor season, finishing in 20th place in the Cheshire County League, just above the bottom two. Sandbach Ramblers finished bottom and did not seek re-election, and Charlie Sandbach also disappeared, his whereabouts subsequently untraced.

Appearances: FL: 2 apps 0 gls Total: 2 apps 0 gls

SHARP, Buchanan 'Kenny'

Inside-forward
5' 11"   12st 9lbs
Born: Alexandria, Dunbartonshire, 2 November 1894
Died: Bolton, 11 January 1956
Career: Vale of Leven Academy. Vale of Leven Juniors. Clydebank Juniors. Chelsea November 1919. Tottenham Hotspur March 1923. Leicester City January 1925. NELSON June 1926. Southport October 1928.
Debut v Wigan Borough (a) 28.8.26, lost 1-2

Kenny Sharp's first season at Seedhill saw the side well in the hunt for promotion. With seven games remaining they were just four points adrift of leaders Stoke City, and they had a game in hand. The Easter period ended all hopes of promotion, however, as the side lost six of its last seven matches and finished in fifth place. Despite a relatively good season, a four-figure loss was announced and a mass exodus of players so severely damaged the team that they finished at the foot of the table in 1927-28. After working so well in tandem with Jimmy Hampson in 1926-27 (both players scoring 23 League goals in 35 matches), his transfer to Blackpool left a gap that proved difficult to fill, and Sharp's effectiveness was diminished as a consequence. Born into a family of thirteen, Kenny Sharp worked in engineering during the First World War and joined Chelsea in November 1919. A great footwork artist with all the touches of a First Division player, he was adept at keeping possession of the ball, and generally parted with it at the right moment. His career ended with just four matches for Southport, scoring in his final outing at Tranmere Rovers. His career aggregate figures were 162 League appearances and 57 goals. He settled in Bolton, where he worked as a machinist at de Havillands.

Appearances: FL: 80 apps 35 gls FAC: 3 apps 1 gl
Total: 83 apps 36 gls

SHEVLIN, Peter

Goalkeeper
5' 9"   11st 4lbs
Born: Wishaw, Lanarkshire, 18 November 1905
Died: Manchester, 10 October 1948
Career: St Mary's (Hamilton). Uddingston St John's. Pollok 1923. St Roch August 1924. Celtic October 1924, fee £120. South Shields July 1927. NELSON September 1929 to March 1931. Shelbourne June 1931, appointed player-manager December 1931. Hamilton Academical (trial) February, professional April 1933. Celtic (loan) May 1934. Albion Rovers May 1935. Hexham Town by February 1937. Jarrow. Chopwell Colliery June 1939.
Debut v Darlington (h) 11.9.29, lost 0-1

At the commencement of season 1929-30, Nelson fielded three different goalkeepers within the space of the first three League engagements. With the 'goals against' tally at that juncture standing at 12, the directors entered the transfer market and recruited Peter Shevlin, widely considered as one of the best goalkeepers in the Northern Section of Division Three. A cool and reliable custodian, Shevlin had spent three seasons with Celtic, gaining a Scottish Cup winner's medal in 1925, and a runners-up award in the following season. Later in his career he missed a third Scottish Cup Final appearance with Hamilton Academical against Rangers when he was injured on the eve of the match and had to stand down. He was very severely wounded during a Midlands

bombing raid in the spring of 1941, and was hospitalised until December of the same year.
Appearances: FL: 53 apps 0 gls FAC: 3 apps 0 gls
Total: 56 apps 0 gls
Honours: Celtic, Scottish Cup winners 1925, finalists 1926.

SIMPSON, Edwin

Left-half 5' 7½" 10st 7lbs
Born: Chilton, County Durham, 21 January 1909
Died: Bishop Middleham, County Durham, 31 August 1973
Career: Chilton Colliery Railway Athletic amateur October 1926. Blackburn Rovers (trial) early March 1927. NELSON 16th March 1927. Crewe Alexandra October 1928. Craghead United. South Moor Colliery August 1934.
Debut v Chesterfield (h) 18.4.27, lost 0–3
Recommended to Nelson by Blackburn Rovers, who had offered the youthful wing half a trial, but felt that he was not potential First Division material. Simpson played in several matches for Nelson reserves and twice in the first team in 1926-27, and commenced the new season as first choice left-half. Although a steady young player with good distribution, Simpson lacked the physique necessary for the rigours of life at the foot of the Northern Section, and he played little first team football beyond mid December. He did not reach senior level during his spell with Crewe Alexandra.
Appearances: FL: 17 apps 0 gls Total: 17 apps 0 gls

SLACK, William

Outside-left
5' 8", 12st 7lbs
Born: Skegby, Nottingham, 20 January 1906
Died: Skegby, Nottingham, 9 August 1989
Career: Sutton Junction cs 1924. Shirebrook January 1927. Sutton Junction March 1927. Blackpool May 1927, fee £125. NELSON March 1928. Portsmouth August 1928. Merthyr Town June 1929. Norwich City May 1930. Mansfield Town August 1932. Sutton Town cs 1936. Ripley Town February 1937.
Debut v Hartlepools United (a) 17.3.28, won 5–4 (scored one).
A wingman built more on the lines of a full-back, Bill Slack made his Football League debut with Nelson and marked it with a stunning goal. A fine sprint and centre from Billy Bottrill was met on the volley by Slack, leaving Brown, the Hartlepools goalkeeper, helpless. The burly wingman departed Seedhill after the briefest of stays, but he did not reach senior level with Portsmouth. On the move again, he joined Merthyr Town who finished at the foot of the Third Division South, having conceded 135 goals in what proved to be their final season as a Football League club. A move to Norwich City failed to improve his fortunes, as the Canaries also finished at the bottom of the Southern Section in his first season. A final homeward move in League circles took him to Mansfield Town. Born only a few miles from Field Mill, he enjoyed four seasons with the Stags who successfully converted him from outside-left to left-half. Bill Slack made a career total of 201 League appearances, and he scored 11 goals. During Army service he represented Western Command against the RAF.
Appearances: FL: 10 apps 3 gls Total: 10 apps 3 gls

SMITH, Frederick

Inside-forward 5' 8" 10st 10lbs
Born: Blackburn, *circa* 1901
Career: Blackburn Rovers May 1922. Barnoldswick Town (trial) July 1924. NELSON November 1924. Fleetwood August 1926. Darwen. William Dickinson & Son (Blackburn) amateur November 1932.
Debut v Southport (h) 21.4.25, won 2–1
Three days after a disappointing defeat at Wrexham by 4 goals to 2, a Nelson side showing three changes beat Southport in a top-of-the-table clash at Seedhill. Fred Smith was introduced at inside-left in place of Edgar Chadwick, and although lacking in experience he had the satisfaction of laying on the first of Fred Laycock's two goals, in what proved to be Nelson's final victory of the campaign. Successive defeats at Rotherham County and Durham City rounded off a season when the team had challenged strongly for promotion but finished second to Darlington, who took the Northern Section title and, with it, the one available promotion place.
Appearances: FL: 1 app 0 gls Total: 1 apps 0 gls

SPARGO, Stephen

Wing-half 5' 11½" 10st 12lbs
Born: Burnley, 29 December 1903
Died: Burnley, April quarter 1972
Career: Mount Olivet FC. Burnley amateur November, professional December 1924. NELSON July 1929. Doncaster Rovers September 1930. York City August 1932. Rochdale September 1933. Burton Town September 1934.
Debut v Darlington (h) 11.9.29, lost 0–1

A product of Burnley Sunday School League football who understudied the Claret's captain and centre-half Jack Hill in a lengthy spell at Turf Moor. The 'Lancashire Daily Post Annual 1926-27' considered that Spargo was one of the most promising junior centre-half backs in the Central League. It was, however, in the Northern Section of Division Three that he eventually found his level, although with Nelson the opportunity to follow the veteran international George Wilson at centre-half was denied him, as he was mainly fielded at wing half. He subsequently enjoyed good spells with Doncaster Rovers (48 matches) and York City (35 matches) but played only four times for Rochdale before moving into non-League football.

Appearances: FL: 21 apps 0 gls FAC: 1 app 0 gls
Total: 22 apps 0 gls

SPENCE, George Robert

Outside-right
Born: Burnley, 6 April 1904
Career: Colne Town. NELSON amateur 8th October, professional 21st October 1927. Rossendale United June 1928. Great Harwood January 1929. B. Thornber's Sports (Burnley) amateur October 1929. A. Cuerdale's Mill (Burnley) amateur April 1932. Accrington Road Unity amateur October 1933.
Debut v Chesterfield (h) 8.10.27, drawn 3–3

Two new amateur players made their first appearance in League football in Nelson's home match versus Chesterfield. Walter Bossons, ex Macclesfield Town, was in goal, and George Spence, recruited on the day of his debut from Colne Town, was at outside-right. Both acquitted themselves well in the 3–3 draw. Spence holding his place for a run of eight matches, in the course of which he scored against Hartlepools United and Ashington. Thereafter he was given few opportunities in a side that finished at the foot of the Northern section.

Appearances: FL: 13 apps 2 gls FAC: 1 app 0 gls
Total: 14 apps 2 gls

STEEL, John Hay

Full-back
5' 8" 11st 2lbs
Born: Glasgow, circa 1895
Died: Cathcart, 1 April 1953, age 58
Career: Queen's Park August 1919. Third Lanark May 1920. NELSON July 1921, fee £150. Arthurlie cs 1924. Arsenal (trial) December 1924. Brentford January 1925 to May 1926.
Debut v Wigan Borough (h) 27.8.21, lost 1–2

John Steel was said to have improved perceptively during his season at Hampden Park with the Queen's Park club, where he made his debut against Clydebank on 20th August 1919 and went on to record 38 League and three Scottish Cup matches in his single season with the famous amateurs. He took the professional ticket with Third Lanark for season 1920-21 and made 12 Scottish League appearances as cover for regular backs McCormack and Orr. He arrived at Seedhill in July 1921, being one of player-manager David Wilson's early signings from across the border. A capable defender whose only fault was a tendency to hold onto the ball for too long, he was unfortunate to suffer a cartilage injury in his first season. He was operated upon but was unable to reclaim the left-back position when fit due to Clem Rigg's outstanding displays. He was, however, fielded as a half-back and at outside-left before the end of the season, filling both roles with equal faculty. Although commencing the championship-winning season in reserve, Steel regained his first team place at right full-back at the expense of Bob Lilley, and partnered Clem Rigg in 26 matches in his final season. He was most unfortunate to develop knee trouble and was unable to take his place in Nelson's continental tour in May 1924. Briefly associated with Arthurlie after leaving Seedhill, Steel was brought south by Arsenal for trials before winding up his senior career with Brentford. When not playing football, John Steel worked as a butcher.

Appearances: 50 apps 0 gls FAC: 2 apps 0 gls Total: 52 apps 0 gls

Honours: Nelson, Third Division North champions 1923.

STEVENSON, John Alexander

Inside-left
5' 7½" 10st 8lbs
Born: Wigan, 27 February 1898
Died: Carlisle, 12 March 1979
Career: Kilbirnie Ladeside. Sunderland (trial). Ayr United July 1920. Aberdeen May 1921, fee £50. Beith cs 1922. Bury (trial) March, professional May 1923. NELSON March 1925, fee £500. St Johnstone June 1927. Falkirk July 1930. Chester August 1932. Bristol Rovers February 1933. Motherwell (trial). Carlisle United June 1933 to 1935.
Debut v Lincoln City (a) 18.3.25, lost 1–2 (scored)

In terms of English League football alone, John Stevenson scored 41 goals in 165 League matches for five different clubs. After leaving Nelson he had excellent spells with both St Johnstone and Falkirk, boosting his overall career figures to 329 matches and 74 goals. Although his arrival at Seedhill, on transfer deadline day in March 1925, failed to lift the side sufficiently to win promotion – they finished second to Darlington – Stevenson was immediately impressive. Considered the teams' outstanding forward, his shrewd and polished displays featured accurate ball control and distribution, and he was always dangerous in front of goal. His most outstanding season proved to be his last at Seedhill. The team finished in fifth place, scoring 104 League goals in 42 matches, Stevenson netting 17 goals, Hampson and Sharp 23 each. The team were never so prolific again, indeed they finished at the foot of table in 1927-28 and a similar placing in 1930-31 resulted in their failure to gain re-election to the Football League. John Stevenson's father was Sunderland's regular right-half in season 1889-90, the last season prior to the club's elevation to the Football League. John's brother, George, was a quite exceptionally talented inside-forward who won 12 Scottish caps during a lengthy spell of 16 seasons with Motherwell (1923 to the War) during which time he scored 169 League goals in 510 matches,

Appearances: FL: 73 apps 26 gls FAC: 2 apps 2 gls Total: 75 apps 28 gls

STONEHAM, John

Goalkeeper 6' 3" 12st 7lbs
Born: Carlisle
Career: Border Regiment. Carlisle United August 1920. Sunderland May 1923. NELSON June 1927 to January 1928.
Debut v Accrington Stanley (h) 27.8.27, lost 1–4

Nelson fielded four different goalkeepers in season 1927-28, and each one of them stepped into the firing line – with a vengeance - in a season when 136 goals were conceded in 42 League matches. This total, incidentally, is the second highest 'goals against' recorded in a Football League season. Darwen, of Division Two, hold the dubious record of conceding 141 in season 1898-99. The ideally built Stoneham assisted Carlisle United to win the North-Eastern League championship in season 1921-22, but spent much of his Sunderland spell as understudy to the legendary England international goalkeeper Albert McInroy. Despite commencing as first choice with Nelson, Stoneham was again cast as understudy, this time to Sam Warhurst. His final appearance for Nelson, and in League football, on 12th November 1927, was captured for posterity on a Gallaher's cigarette card, depicting action from the Bradford City v Nelson match. This can have been of little consolation to the shell-shocked custodian as Nelson were most comprehensively walloped 9–1. Considering the fact that in his

previous outing, against Manchester City in the Lancashire Senior Cup, Stoneham had been on the receiving end of a 10–2 blitzkrieg, it was not surprising that he requested a transfer. As the local correspondent tactfully commented "It would be mutually advantageous if he could go elsewhere."
Appearances: FL: 6 apps 0 gls Total: 6 apps 0 gls

SUTTIE, David Shand

Left-half 5' 8" 11st 0lbs
Born: Lochgelly, Fife, 18 December 1906
Died: Blackburn, 30 April 1985
Career: Blackburn Rovers amateur 1926, professional June 1927. NELSON August 1928. Manchester Central June 1931. Ashton National May 1932. Carlisle United September 1933. Stalybridge Celtic February 1935.
Debut v Lincoln City (h) 25.9.28, lost 3–4
The son of Thomas Suttie, a Blackburn Rovers full-back in pre-WW1 days, David also joined the Rovers, but despite earning a professional contract, he did not feature at senior level. Although he commenced at reserve team level with Nelson he was quickly given his chance in the League side and grasped his opportunity, scoring twice in 28 League matches in his first season. Although the club's fortunes were in serious decline during his three years at Seedhill, Suttie's contribution could not be faulted. On either flank in the middle line he worked extremely hard throughout ninety minutes, and his shrewd distribution continually put his forward colleagues into action.
Appearances: FL: 104 apps 2 gls FAC: 4 apps 0 gls Total: 108 apps 2 gls

TAYLOR, Harold 'Harry'

Outside-left 5' 10" 11st 0lbs
Born: Ripley
Career: Ripley Town. NELSON amateur August 1926, professional January 1927. Mossley
Debut v Lincoln City (h) 26.2.27, won 2–1
The transfer of Edwin Earle to Burnley in December 1926 gave reserve wingman Harry Taylor an opportunity, but he failed to capitalise and experienced outside-left Lewis Bedford was signed from Walsall prior to the transfer deadline. Taylor meanwhile had done enough at reserve level to earn a contract for the following season and in mid term he enjoyed an extended run in the side after Lewis Bedford had been transferred back to Walsall. In scanning the 'Lancashire Daily Post Annuals' for seasons 1926-27 and 1927-28, it was noted that Taylor had lost half a stone in twelve months, what was less clear was how his height had also been reduced from 5' 10" to 5' 6½" in the same period!
Appearances: FL: 17 Apps 4 gls Total: 17 apps 4 gls

TEBB, Thomas Edward

Inside-forward 5' 9" 11st 7lbs
Born: Westerhope, Newcastle-on-Tyne, January quarter 1911
Died: Westerhope, Newcastle-on-Tyne, 23 June 1957
Career: Scotswood circa 1927. Aston Villa (trial). Hull City (trial). Washington Colliery August 1929. NELSON July 1930. Wigan Borough July 1931. Lancaster Town July 1932. Tottenham Hotspur June 1933. Northfleet United (loan) August 1933. Blyth Spartans December 1934.
Debut v Rochdale (a) 30.8.30, lost 4–5
Tommy Tebb played for Scotswood FC at 16 years of age, and at 17 was selected to play for The Rest of the North-Eastern League v the Champions (Sunderland Reserves). A sprinter of some repute, he was first associated with Lancashire football when he joined Nelson and, a season later, Wigan Borough, up to the winding-up of that club. When signed by Lancaster Town in August 1932, the local press commented: "He is made of the right stuff, possessing the grit of the colliery district on the banks of the Tyne". In May 1933 he was linked with a move to Preston North End, but in the following month was signed by Spurs. In mid season he returned homewards to join Blyth Spartans after a wealth of experience while still in his prime at just 23 years of age.
Appearances: FL: 14 apps 2 gls Total: 14 apps 2 gls

THOMSON, John

Goalkeeper 6' 0" 12st 6lbs
Born: Dundee, circa 1897
Career: Shettleston. Dundee August 1920. Gillingham June 1921. Barrow June 1923. NELSON March 1924, fee 'about £500'. Benburb August 1927. Cork City trainer July 1931.
Debut v Barnsley (a) 15.3.24, drawn 0–0
Signed as emergency cover for Harry Abbott in late season 1923-24, ideally proportioned goalkeeper John Thomson first crossed the border in 1921 to play with Gillingham. He spent two seasons with the Kentish club before losing his place to Fred Fox. In

the summer he trekked north to join Barrow where he shared first team duties with Norman Wharton. Said to have cost Nelson, battling for Second Division survival, a significant sum, he was called upon only twice for first team duty. As the side took three points from the matches in which he played, successive fixtures against Barnsley, he was not found wanting, but the team's form dipped in the final weeks of the campaign. One win in the final seven fixtures condemned the side to relegation after just one season in Division Two.
Appearances: FL: 2 apps 0 gls Total: 2 apps 0 gls

TORDOFF, Harry

Centre-half 5' 8½" 12st 0lbs
Born: Barnsley, 25 November 1905
Died: Sheffield, July quarter 1976
Career: NELSON amateur May, professional September 1929. Sheffield United February 1930, along with Harry Hooper for a combined fee of £750. Rotherham United June 1931. Boston Town (trial) September 1932. Barnsley July 1933. Worksop Town June 1934.
Debut v Accrington Stanley (a) 4.5.29, drawn 4–4
Injuries to George Wilson and James Metcalfe opened the way for Harry Tordoff to secure a place in Nelson's first team in January 1930. The well built central defender stepped up well, but it was something of a surprise when he was transferred to First Division Sheffield United after just a handful of League appearances. Rumours in the town had linked Harry Hooper with a move to the Blades, but it was totally unexpected when it was learned that Harry Tordoff was to accompany him to Bramall Lane. While Hooper flourished in the top flight, Tordoff did not develop as expected, failing to reach first team level, and he subsequently appeared only twice more in League football.
Appearances: FL: 9 apps 0 gls Total: 9 apps 0 gls

TURNER, Albert James

Right-half 5' 10" 11st 0lbs
Born: Blackpool, 7 April 1901
Died: Blackpool, 24 April 1985
Career: South Shore. NELSON amateur April 1922. Lytham October 1923.
Debut v Halifax Town (a) 8.4.22, lost 1–3
Albert Turner's solitary Football League appearance was made in atrocious conditions, for a heavy fall of rain and sleet turned Halifax Town's pitch into a quagmire. Snow fell heavily toward the end of the game in which Nelson failed to open out the play and were well beaten. Wooton's goal, scored moments before the final whistle was too little, too late, for Nelson who found themselves only three points above the bottom two places and descending very perilously towards a re-election application in their first season in the Football League.
Appearances: FL: 1 app 0 gls Total: 1 app 0 gls

WALKER, Stanley

Centre-forward
Career: An amateur throughout: NELSON February 1931. Clitheroe. Brierfield Mills July 1931. Brierfield Legion March 1933. Brierfield Old Boys August 1933.
Debut v Accrington Stanley (a) 28.2.31, lost 1–3
Stan Walker's bow in League football was made at Accrington Stanley's Peel Park on a snowy afternoon in late February 1931. Trade depression was playing havoc with attendances throughout all the divisions, and although the game was a local "Derby", the attendance was 2,216, and the "gate" receipts just £77. Introduced from reserve ranks for the first time in preference to Tom Carmedy, Walker could make little headway against Viner, Accrington's experienced centre-half. He did, however, have a goal, that appeared quite a legitimate one, disallowed by the referee. A quite serious injury to Nelson's Arthur Hawes, who missed most of the second half, further disorganised the attack, which was criticised for its inability to hold on the ball – and to score goals.
Appearances: FL: 2 apps 0 gls Total: 2 apps 0 gls

WALLER, William

Inside-left 5' 8½" 11st 6lbs
Born: Bolton, October quarter 1894
Died: Great Lever, 19 November 1985
Career: Horwich RMI. NELSON December 1920, fee £50, registered for FL matches August 1921. Burnley June 1922. Chorley (trial) February 1924. Queens Park Rangers later in February 1924.
Debut v Crewe Alexandra (h) 12.11.21, lost 1–2
Prematurely balding Bill Waller scored 14 Central League goals for Nelson in season 1920-21. His total included hat-tricks against Tranmere Rovers and Southport, and despite have played for only half of the season, he was second highest goal scorer behind Harry Hargeaves, who scored 16. Perhaps unsurprisingly, he found goals harder to come by in the following season, when Nelson made their bow as a Football League club. He did, however, score on his debut against Crewe Alexandra and held his place after displacing Irish international Halligan. An upward move to First Division neighbours Burnley in the close season saw him unable to break into a team that regularly included six internationals, Waller's only first team involvement being a late season debut at Birmingham in a 1–0 defeat.

Appearances: FL: 25 apps 7 gls FAC: 3 apps 3 gls Total: 28 apps 10 gls

WALMSLEY, John William

Centre-half   5' 9½"   12st 4lbs
Born: Accrington, 22 April 1903
Died: Haslingden, October quarter 1970
Career: St Paul's S.S. Accrington St Peter's. Bacup Borough. NELSON February 1921, registered for FL matches August 1921. Barnoldswick Town 1923. Accrington Stanley May 1924. Barnoldswick Town June 1926. Great Harwood July 1929. Horwich RMI 1929. St Ignatius (Preston) amateur October 1929. Howard & Bullough FC amateur October 1930. Higher Walton (Preston) amateur November 1934.
Debut v Wrexham (a) 26.11.21, 2–4

Discovered in Accrington Sunday School football, the curly-haired and hefty utility defender eventually returned to his hometown club and made 17 League appearances for Stanley in two seasons at Peel Park. He was restricted to a single senior outing with Nelson, this coming when the team made their first-ever visit to Wrexham. Although the game ended in defeat, Nelson led 2–1 at the interval and all but the referee felt that Nelson should have had a third goal. Bennie struck a close range shot that hit the underside of the crossbar, the ball appeared to have rebounded well over the line before being scrambled away but the referee's verdict was quite emphatic. Wrexham had the better of the exchanges in the second half, running out deserved winners by 4 - 2
Appearances: FL: 1 app 0 gls Total: 1 app 0 gls

WARD, Edward 'Ted'

Inside-forward
5' 4"   9st 12lbs
Born: Cowpen, 16 June 1896
Career: Blyth Shamrocks. Blyth Spartans April 1913. Bedlington United June 1913. Blyth Spartans August 1919. Newcastle United May 1920, fee £300. Crystal Palace June 1922, fee £250. NELSON July 1923. Darlington December 1924. Ashington August 1925. Workington August 1927. West Stanley August 1928. Carlisle United. Blyth Spartans player-coach October 1930, trainer August 1931.
Debut v Hull City (h) 15.9.23, drawn 1–1

The absence of Sid Hoad and Dick Crawshaw, due to ongoing injury problems, gave Ted Ward his first opportunity at Seedhill, and the game also marked the League debut of Edgar Chadwick. As they entertained Hull City, the team were still without their first victory of the season, having scored only four goals in the first six Second Division matches. On a sunny afternoon, more suited to cricket than football, the experimental forward line showed surprisingly good form, but the Hull goalkeeper was rarely troubled, the old failings in front of goal continuing, Ward spurning two "glorious chances" according to the local correspondent. Earlier in his career, Ward played in 25 League and Cup matches for Newcastle United as they challenged for the FL championship. A persistent knee injury blighted his spell with Crystal Palace and it was not until season 1925-26 that his career took an upturn, when he scored 10 goals in 26 matches for Ashington, the club that his brother, Walter, had assisted some two years earlier.
Appearances: FL: 2 apps 0 gls Total: 2 apps 0 gls

WARHURST, Sam Lee

Goalkeeper   5' 8"   10st 10lbs
Born: Nelson, 29 December 1907
Died: Southampton, 17 February 1981
Career: Nelson British Legion. NELSON amateur October 1926, professional October 1927. Stalybridge Celtic June 1931. Bradford City June 1932. Southampton May 1937; appointed trainer-coach March 1946 to 1952.

Debut v Durham City (h) 24.9.27, won 2–1

Local amateur goalkeeper Sam Warhurst was not possessed of the physique normally associated with his position, but he was usefully elusive once he had gathered the ball, in the days when goalkeeper and ball could be charged through quite legitimately. He graduated through the ranks at Seedhill, commencing with six Lancashire Combination matches, as deputy for Fred Mace, in season 1926-27. Re-signed as reserve goalkeeper for season 1927-28, he took over first team duties from former Sunderland custodian John Stoneham and made 31 League appearances during the season. He then shared the first team jersey with Desmond Fawcett in 1928-29, but played little in the following term when Peter Shevlin missed only five matches. Among the players released in the close season, he was then re-signed in October 1930 and rounded off his Nelson career with 23 League appearances in 1930-31. He returned to League action with Bradford City after a season with Stalybridge Celtic, and made 66 appearances in two seasons at Valley Parade. His final move took him to Southampton where he was the Saints regular goalkeeper until the outbreak of war ended his League career, but he continued to assist the team during wartime football. He was appointed trainer-coach after the war, but left in the wake of the club's relegation from Division Two in 1953. He was then landlord of the St. Mary's Hotel in the town, until its demolition in 1972 to make way for a new shopping centre. At this point, Sam opted for retirement.

Appearances: FL: 76 apps 0 gls FAC: 1 app 0 gls
Total: 77 apps 0 gls

WEEDALL, John Thomas

Outside-left
Born: Bolton, 24 October 1907
Died: Fleetwood, 30 March 1979
Career: NELSON August 1929. Chorley December 1930. Breightmet United. Holden's Temperance (Bolton) October 1933. Breightmet United September 1934.
Debut v Accrington Stanley (a) 24.9.29, lost 0–3

As understudy to Foster Hedley for the left wing berth, John Weedall found few opportunities, and the fact that he failed to secure a regular place in the League side after Hedley moved to Manchester City suggested that he was not considered first team material. He was, however, the possessor of a hard shot, and three goals in his last five outings suggested that he might have been afforded more opportunities in a season when the team was very short of firepower.

Appearances: FL: 7 apps 3 gls Total: 7 apps 3 gls

WHITE, Henry Albert 'Harry'

Inside-forward
5' 8"   11st 7lbs
Born: Watford, 8 August 1895
Died: Barrow Gurney, Somerset, 27 November 1972
Career: Watford Grammar School. Wharncliffe Athletic. Brentford April 1914. Arsenal July 1919. Blackpool March 1923, fee £1,250. Fulham May 1925, fee £500. Walsall February 1926. NELSON March 1927. Walsall October 1927. Stafford Rangers August 1928. Thames Association September 1929. Columbia, Earlsfield, reinstated amateur August 1930. Wimbledon trainer-coach September 1932. Wimbledon Wednesday amateur February 1933. Sutton United trainer-coach July 1938.
Debut v Accrington Stanley 12.3.27, won 7–0 (scored one)

In a brief but very productive stay at Seedhill, White scored in each of his first four matches and netted a hat-trick against Hartlepools United on April 9th, 1927. He joined the Seedhill ranks from Walsall in a double signing, along with outside-left Lewis Bedford. Five years earlier, when successfully leading Arsenal's attack, his attributes were outlined as follows: "White is not a stylist, but he knows where the goal lies, and whenever he gets the ball the goal is always his objective". His form with the Gunners led to his appearance in an international trial match in September 1919, when he played for the South versus the North at Stamford Bridge. His talents were not confined to football. His father, also Harry, was ground superintendent at Lords, and Harry junior played in Minor Counties cricket with Norfolk in 1921 and in County Cricket with Warwickshire as an off-break bowler in 1923. In the following year he coached at Charterhouse School. During World War One he served in the Royal Fusiliers, and he later coached Essex Amateur FA and was groundsman at Brentwood School.

Appearances: FL: 22 apps 15 gls Total: 22 apps 15 gls

WILD, Robert Durham

Right-half   5' 8"   12st 0lbs
Born: Windhill, New Shipley, October quarter 1895
Career: Bradford City amateur April 1914. Wartime guest player with Hull City March 1917. Bradford City professional 1919. NELSON June 1921. Halifax Town September 1922. Barnoldswick Town October 1924.
Debut v Wigan Borough (h) 27.8.21, lost 1–2

Bob Wild made his Football League debut in the First Division for Bradford City against Liverpool at Anfield on 6th September 1919. He had played regularly, however, during wartime seasons 1917-18 and 1918-19. He was one of a number of experienced players to swell the Seedhill ranks for their first season in League football, and an early match report left no doubt that he was among the best of the new signings: "Wild captivated the eye by his neat footwork at left-half, pleasing the quidnuncs immensely". Despite missing only two first team matches throughout the season, Wild was on the move after just one term, linking with Halifax Town where he spent his final two seasons of senior football. His last season at the Shay was memorable for the team's wonderful run in the FA Cup competition when they progressed to the second round proper for the first time. Peterborough & Fletton United and Rotherham County were both beaten 1–0 in the qualifying rounds. It took two replays to overcome Northampton Town in the first round proper, Bob Wild scoring a rare goal in the second replay, won 4–2 by the Shaymen. The reward was a visit to First Division giants Manchester City who, quite sensationally, were twice held to draws before a second replay at Old Trafford finally ended the dream, City winning 3–0.

Appearances: FL: 36 apps 0 gls FAC: 3 apps 0 gls Total: 39 apps 0 gls

WILKINSON, Thomas

Inside-left   5' 9"   11st 7lbs
Born: Newfield, County Durham, 8 February 1902
Career: Beamish Athletic. Tanfield Lea Institute. Pelton Fell Institute. Hull City November 1924. Chester-le-Street August 1926. Blyth Spartans December 1926. Everton May 1927. NELSON July 1928. Twizzell United. Annfield Plain January 1929. Craghead United February 1929. Shildon September 1930. Beamish Athletic March 1932. Lumley United September 1932. Consett October 1932. Beamish Rovers September 1935.
Debut v Hartlepools United (a) 25.8.28, drawn 2–2

Tom Wilkinson made his Football League debut with Hull City in a 1–0 defeat at Leicester City on 28th March 1925, but made only a further three League appearances and, despite scoring twice, a season in non-League football followed. His year with Everton was spent in reserve team football, and he spent just half a season with Nelson, rather surprisingly returning homewards after missing just three first team matches during his brief stay.

Appearances: FL: 17 apps 5 gls Total: 17 apps 5 gls

WILSON, David

Half-back   5' 8"   12st 6lbs
Born: Irvine, Ayrshire, 14 January 1884
Career: Irvine Meadow. St. Mirren 1902-03. Hamilton Academical August 1904. Bradford City November 1904. Oldham Athletic May 1906, fee £90. Wartime guest player with Stockport County April 1917. Appointed Oldham Athletic player-coach September 1920. NELSON player-manager May 1921, manager only from May 1924 to cs 1925. Exeter City manager March 1928 to February 1929.
Debut v Wigan Borough (h) 27.8.21, lost 1–2

David Wilson was one of a family of footballers, whose ranks included elder brother Andrew, a Scottish International centre-forward with Sheffield Wednesday; James (St. Mirren and Preston North End) and Alex (Preston North End and Oldham Athletic). David's career began in Scottish League football at the age of eighteen, and he commenced in the Football League in December 1904, when he made his first appearance for Bradford City in a 2–0 defeat at Blackpool. After 12 appearances and one goal he joined Oldham Athletic, at that time a Lancashire Combination club. In his second season the Latics gained entry into Division Two of the Football League, and Wilson was one of the driving forces in a side that came within a whisker of clinching the Football League Championship in 1914-15, Everton taking the title by the narrow margin of one point. Several records were broken by the tireless and enthusiastic wing-half, who was capped by Scotland in 1913. In League and Cup matches alone he totalled 180 consecutive outings, and in all games, including minor cup matches and friendly fixtures he appeared in 263 consecutive matches. His lengthy association with Oldham Athletic ended when he accepted the post of player-manager to Nelson, for their debut in the Third Division Northern Section. All roads led to Seedhill for Nelson's opening fixture against Wigan Borough and it took just two minutes for Irish International Bill Halligan to give the home side the lead. Sadly, they were unable to protect their early advantage and were defeated by a 2–1 score line. The side's form remained patchy throughout their first season despite the best efforts of the player-manager whose experience, sound judgment and tuition hauled the side clear of the re-election zone and to the relative safety of 16*th* place in the table. With a season's experience behind him, and many new faces recruited, a more settled line-up included the best of the season's imports: Birds (Stockport County), Braidwood (Oldham Athletic), Broadhead (Scunthorpe & Lindsay United), Wolstenholme (Darlington), McCulloch (Heart of Midlothian) and Hutchinson (Ashington). Promotion to Division Two was achieved, and a trip to Spain undertaken in the close season. Quite remarkably, Real Madrid were beaten 4–2, Nelson's scorers on the famous occasion being Eddleston, Hutchinson and Crawshaw (2). During the close season the club's directors proceeded with an ambitious ground improvement and extension scheme, the playing pitch being considerably enlarged and a new stand erected. All of the previous season's championship side were retained, and a reserve side was entered into the Lancashire Combination. Hovering around the dreaded relegation places throughout, their fate was settled on the last day of the season, and this despite a 3–1 victory against the season's champions, Leeds United, other results leaving Nelson in 21st place. At the age of forty, Wilson retired as a player, but continued as manager for one more season, during which he came frustratingly short of regaining the lost Second Division status, Nelson ending the campaign in second place behind Darlington, when only one team was promoted from the Northern Section. In the close season Wilson resigned and spent some years out of football, running his own stocks and shares business in Blackpool. He returned to the game as Exeter City's manager in March 1928, but after a run of six consecutive defeats, club and manager parted company, with some love lost, on St. Valentine's Day 1929.

Appearances: FL: 95 apps 3 gls FAC: 7 apps 0 gls
Total: 102 apps 3 gls

Honours: Scotland International, one cap v England in 1913. Nelson, Third Division North champions 1923.

WILSON, George

Centre-half
5' 10"   11st 0lbs
Born: Blackpool, 14 January 1892
Died: Blackpool, 25 November 1961
Career: Sacred Heart School. Preston Schoolboys. Catholic College (Preston). Willows Rovers. Stanley Villa. Fleetwood amateur. Willows Rovers. Morecambe 1911. Blackpool amateur December 1911, professional January 1912. Sheffield Wednesday March 1920, fee £3,000. NELSON July 1925, fee £2,000, a then record fee paid by a Third Division club. Retired July 1930.
Debut v Crewe Alexandra (h) 29.8.25, won 2–1

George Wilson began in junior football as a forward, and eventually found his way to Blackpool after playing in just five games at centre-forward for Morecambe. A faltering start in Blackpool's reserves took an upturn when he scored his first goal against Manchester United reserves at Bloomfield Road, and, on the evening of the match, he signed his first professional contract. He made his League debut in the following month at Leeds City. In a 1922 interview, Wilson admitted that his career was going nowhere until Blackpool's assistant trainer George Anderson, a one time famous centre-half of Blackburn Rovers, suggested to the directors of the club that Wilson would make an ideal centre-half. Despite a 5–0 thrashing at Derby County in his first outing in the new position Wilson maintained his place until the war put a stop to his football. In France and Belgium he had little opportunity to play, but in the more serious business, he was awarded the Belgium Medal of Honour for bravery in action. Returning to Blackpool after the war he was elected captain, but in March 1920 he was surprisingly transfer listed, and Sheffield Wednesday splashed out a club record fee to take him to Hillsborough. In five seasons he accumulated 196 League and Cup appearances, and despite operating in a Second Division team that failed to rise above mid table, he was awarded 12 full England Caps, captaining his country on several occasions, and he additionally represented the Football League in five matches. He was awarded a benefit of £650 at the close of the 1924-25 season, but following a dispute over terms for a new contract he departed Hillsborough and, to the amazement of the football world, joined Nelson for a fee that constituted a record for a Third Division club. Elected captain on arrival at Seedhill, he was the most conspicuous player in the side. Said to use his head, in more ways than one, he showed wonderful ability and resource, and a feature of his game was his ability to springboard attacks with his accurate use of the ground pass out to the wing. George Wilson announced his retirement at the age of 38, after playing only 12 matches in his final season. As was the case with many footballers of his generation, he worked as a licensee both in Nelson and finally in Blackpool, where he sadly died, very shortly after retiring in 1961.

Appearances: FL: 160 apps 18 gls FAC: 4 apps 0 gls
Total: 164 apps 18 gls
Honours: England International, 12 caps 1921-24. Football League representative, 4 appearances.

WILSON, William 'Billy'

Outside-right   5' 5"   9st 6lbs
Born: Burnley, January quarter 1899
Career: NELSON amateur August 1921. Morecambe September 1923.
Debut v Ashington (h) 14.1.22, lost 0-2

Nelson were said to have fielded "a scratch eleven" for the visit of Ashington, for at the last moment both John Bennie and Joe Eddleston had to cry off due to influenza. Light-weight local amateur Billy Wilson was brought in at outside-right but with the team considered to be "A thoroughly disorganised force", no one was spared the criticism of the local reporter who considered that "Unless the directors can introduce some skilful new wing men, one is afraid that the club will go from bad to worse". Described as "The baby of the party", Billy Wilson was a surprise inclusion in the Nelson squad that toured Spain in the summer of 1923.

Appearances: FL: 1 app 0 gls Total: 1 app 0 gls

WOLSTENHOLME, Arthur

Inside-forward   5' 8"   12st 0lbs
Born: Middleton, 14 May 1889
Died: Manchester, January quarter 1958
Career: Tonge FC. Oldham Athletic March 1908. Blackpool December 1909. Gillingham August 1912. Norwich City July 1913. Lincoln City July 1914. Wartime guest with Oldham Athletic 1915. Oldham Athletic May 1919, fee £75. Newport County June 1920. Darlington June 1921. NELSON May 1922, appointed to training staff season 1923-24, coach July 1925. Colne Town September 1926.
Debut v Bradford Park Avenue (a) 26.8.22, lost 2-6

Arthur Wolstenholme began with Oldham Athletic while still in his teens, scoring ten goals in 26 League appearances in 1908-09. After losing his first team place in the following year he made the first of his many subsequent moves, changing clubs on an annual basis at either side of World War One. He was the first player to score four goals in a Third Division North match when Darlington netted seven against Chesterfield on 10th September 1921, and he went on to score 17 goals in 29 League appearances in the same season when the Quakers finished runners-up to Stockport County for the championship. Nelson's player-manager David Wilson was a former playing colleague during his time with Oldham Athletic, so was well aware of Wolstenholme's qualities. Able to occupy any number of positions, he was a brainy player, not as speedy as in days of yore, but his ripe experience was a valuable asset to the side, and he was very adapt at making openings for his colleagues. 13 goals in 36

League matches was his excellent contribution in Nelson's Third Division North championship side in 1922-23, and he continued at Seedhill in a coaching capacity when his lengthy playing career ended.

Appearances: FL: 68 apps 17 gls FAC: 3 apps 1 gl Total: 71 apps 18 gls

Honours: Nelson, Third Division North champions 1923.

WOOTTON, James

Outside-left   5' 7"   11st 0lbs
Born: Bloxwich, Walsall, July quarter 1895
Died: St Asaph, July quarter 1960, age 65
Career: Leek Alexandra. Wartime guest player with Walsall and Port Vale. Port Vale August 1919. Nuneaton Town July 1921. NELSON January 1922, fee £75. Hereford United. Rugby Town August 1926. Oakengates Town August 1927. Walsall Early Closers amateur August 1932.
Debut v Hartlepools United (h) 21.1.22, lost 0–4

James Wootton signed his first professional contract with Port Vale in August 1919, after making guest appearances for them during the First World War. He saw a fair amount of Division Two football (43 matches and two goals) before moving into non-League circles with Nuneaton Town for season 1921-22. He returned to League action with Nelson, who paid a small fee for his services in January 1922. Life in Division Three North was proving difficult for the Seedhill club, with the outside-left position causing particular concern, four different players having been tried and discarded prior to Wootton's arrival. Despite a couple of heavy defeats by Hartlepools United in his first two matches – 4–0 at Seedhill and 6–1 in the return at Victoria Park – things improved, a 'double' against Southport immediately following. A season that saw the side hovering anxiously just above the bottom two places ended in the relative comfort of 16th place, but moves were made to strengthen the weak places in the side. A large turnover of playing staff in the close season brought many new faces to the Nelson team and James Wootton was among several of the departed who did not feature again in senior football.

Appearances: FL: 14 apps 1 gl Total: 14 apps 1 gl

NOTES ON THE APPEARANCE GRIDS

Home games are shown with the opponent's name in upper case. Nelson's score is always shown first.

League attendances to 1924-25 are as reported at the time. Those for 1925-26 onwards are official figures as recorded by the Football League. Some attendances prior to 1925 have not been found.

Nelson did not play in the FA Cup of 1928-29 since they forgot to enter by the required date.

1921-22

16th in Division Three (North)

#	Date	Opponent	Score	Scorers	Att	Andrews HGR	Baird R	Bennie J	Bruce R	Clegg H	Eddleston J	Halligan W	Hargreaves H	Heyes H	Hoad SJ	Jacques TE	Lilley R	Marsh CA	McGreevy W	Price J	Proctor W	Rigg C	Steel JH	Turner AJ	Waller W	Walmsley JW	Wilde R	Wilson D	Wilson W	Wootton J
1	Aug 27	WIGAN BOROUGH	1-2	Halligan	12000	8					7	9	10	1			2	4			11		3				6	5		
2	Sep 3	Wigan Borough	4-1	Halligan, Hargreaves, Marsh, Jacques	8000						7	9	10	1		4	2	8			11		3				6	5		
3	10	Lincoln City	2-0	Halligan, Hargreaves	9000						7	9	10	1		4	3	8			11		2				6	5		
4	12	STALYBRIDGE CELTIC	1-0	Proctor	9000						7	9	10	1		4	2	8			11		3				6	5		
5	17	LINCOLN CITY	0-0		8000						7	9	10	1		4	2	8			11		3				6	5		
6	24	Darlington	1-0	Halligan	10000						7	9	10	1		4	2	8			11		3				6	5		
7	Oct 1	DARLINGTON	1-1	Eddleston	10000						9		10	1		4	2	8			11		3				6	5		
8	8	Accrington Stanley	1-4	Halligan	14000						7	9	10	1		4	2	8			11	3					6	5		
9	15	ACCRINGTON STANLEY	0-1		12000					1	7		10			5	2	8			11	3					4	6		
10	22	Chesterfield	2-1	Eddleston 2	6000			9	1		7	10	8			5	2				11	3					4	6		
11	29	CHESTERFIELD	2-0	Marsh, Eddleston	5000				1		9	10	8			5	2	7			11	3					4	6		
12	Nov 5	Crewe Alexandra	1-2	Eddleston	5000				1		9	10	8			5	2	7			11	3					4	6		
13	12	CREWE ALEXANDRA	1-2	Chorlton (og)	8000				1		8	10	11			5	2	7				3		9			4	6		
14	26	Wrexham	2-4	Waller, Bennie	6000			9	1		7	8				5	2				11	3			10	5	4	6		
15	Dec 24	Barrow	2-0	Eddleston, Bennie	5000			9	1		7	8				5	2	11				3			10		4	6		
16	26	DURHAM CITY	3-5	Andrews, Bennie, Waller		8		9	1		7					5	2	11				3			10		4	6		
17	27	Stalybridge Celtic	0-2		6000	8		9		1	7					5		11				3	2		10			6		
18	31	Ashington	0-4		5000	8		11		1	7	9				5	2					3	4		10		6			
19	Jan 2	WREXHAM	4-0	Waller, Eddleston, Bennie 2				9			7			1			2	11	5			3	4		10		6	8		
20	14	ASHINGTON	0-2		3000	9								1			2	8	5			3	6		10		4		7	
21	21	HARTLEPOOLS UNITED	0-4		4000			8			9			1	7		2		5			3	6		10		4			11
22	28	Hartlepools United	1-6	Eddleston	7000		7	9			8			1					5			3	2		10		4	6		11
23	Feb 4	SOUTHPORT	3-2	Eddleston, D Wilson (p), Bennie	4000		7	9			8			1					5			3	2		10		4	6		11
24	11	Southport	1-0	Eddleston	4000			9			8			1	7		2		5			3	2		10		4	6		11
25	18	STOCKPORT COUNTY	2-2	Halligan, Waller	8000						8	9		1	7		2		5			3			10		4	6		11
26	25	Stockport County	0-3		12000						9	8		1	7		2		5			3			10		4	6		11
27	Mar 4	GRIMSBY TOWN	3-0	Waller 2, Eddleston	7000	8					9			1	7		2		5			3	11		10		4	6		
28	11	Grimsby Town	1-3	Eddleston		8					9			1	7		2		5			3	11		10		4	6		
29	18	Walsall	0-2		5500	8					9			1	7		2		5			3	11		10		4	6		
30	Apr 1	HALIFAX TOWN	0-0		7000			9			8			1	7		2		5		11	3			10		4	6		
31	8	Halifax Town	1-3	Wootton				9			8			1	7		2		5			3		4	10			6		11
32	14	Durham City	0-2		1000						9			1	7		2		5			3	6		10		4	8		11
33	15	Rochdale	2-2	Eddleston, D Wilson	3000						9			1	7		2		5			3	6		10		4	8		11
34	17	BARROW	1-1	McGreevy							9			1	7		2		5	10		3	6				4	8		11
35	22	ROCHDALE	4-1	Eddleston 3, D Wilson							9			1	7		2		5			3	6		10		4	8		11
36	25	WALSALL	1-0	Waller	3000					1	9					7	6	2	5			3			10		4	8		11
37	29	Tranmere Rovers	0-4		3000					1	9					7	2		5		8	3	6		10		4			11
38	May 6	TRANMERE ROVERS	0-0								9			1	7		2		5		8	6			3		4	5		11

Played in one game: E Eastwood (game 7, at 7), H Mellor (9, at 9),
T Garnett (20, at 11), R Hartley (17, at 4)

	Apps	8	2	12	7	5	37	13	17	13	26	16	17	34	17	3	20	14	29	25	1	25	1	36	34	1	14
	Goals	1		6			16	6	2				1		2	1		1				7			3		1

Two own goals

F.A. Cup

#	Date	Opponent	Score	Scorers	Att																									
Q4	Nov 19	Accrington Stanley	1-0	Waller	10106				1		8	10				5	2	7			11	3		9			4	6		
Q5	Dec 3	ROCHDALE	3-2	Waller, Eddleston, Lilley (p)	6000			9	1		7	8				5	2				11	3			10		4	6		
Q6	17	Worksop Town	1-2	Waller	5000			9	1		7	8				5	2	11				3			10		4	6		

75

1922-23

Champions of Division Three (North): Promoted

#	Date		Opponent	Score	Scorers	Att	Abbott H	Bennett W	Birds J	Black JR	Braidwood JE	Broadhead JE	Crawshaw RL	Eastwood E	Eddleston J	Hoad SJ	Howson C	Hutchinson R	Lilley R	McCulloch MJ	Price J	Rigg C	Steel JH	Wilson D	Wolstenholme AE
1	Aug 26		Bradford Park Avenue	2-6	Eddleston, Howie (og)	10000		1			4	6			9	7		11	2	10	5	3			8
2	Sep 2		BRADFORD PARK AVE.	1-0	McCulloch	7000		1			5	6			9	7		11	2	10		3		4	8
3		9	STALYBRIDGE CELTIC	1-0	Eddleston	5000		1			5	6			9	7		11	2	10		3		4	8
4		12	HALIFAX TOWN	2-0	Eddleston 2	5000		1			5	6			9	7		11	2	10		3		4	8
5		16	Stalybridge Celtic	0-2				1			5	6			9	7		11	2	10		3		4	8
6		23	SOUTHPORT	2-0	McCulloch 2	7500		1	7		5	6			9			11	2	10		3		4	8
7		30	Southport	1-0	Eddleston	5000		1	7		5	6			9			11	2	10		3		4	8
8	Oct 7		ASHINGTON	1-3	Wolstenholme	7000		1	7		5	6			9		2	11	3	10				4	8
9		14	Ashington	2-0	McCulloch, Eddleston	8000		1	7		5	6			9			11	2	10		3		4	8
10		21	Tranmere Rovers	2-0	Eddleston 2	6000		1	7		5	6			9			11	2	10		3		4	8
11		28	TRANMERE ROVERS	1-0	Black	7000		1	7	5	6				9			11		10		3	2	4	8
12	Nov 4		Barrow	0-1		4000		1	7	5	6				9			11		10		3	2	4	8
13		11	BARROW	2-1	Wolstenholme, Eddleston	7000		1	7	5	6				9			11		10		3	2	4	8
14		25	ROCHDALE	1-2	Braidwood	6000	8	1	7	5	6				9			11		10	4	3	2		
15	Dec 9		Darlington	3-2	Braidwood, Eddleston 2	5583		1		5	6				9	7		11		10		3	2	4	8
16		23	DARLINGTON	3-0	Wolstenholme 3	3000		1		5	6				9	7		11		10		3	2	4	8
17		25	Halifax Town	2-2	Braidwood, Wolstenholme	18000		1		5	6				9	7		11		10		3	2	4	8
18		30	HARTLEPOOLS UNITED	4-1	Eddleston, Wolstenholme 2, McCulloch	5000		1		5	6				9	7		11		10		3	2	4	8
19	Jan 6		Hartlepools United	1-5	Wolstenholme	5500		1		5	6				9	7		11		10		3	2	4	8
20		13	Rochdale	3-0	Eddleston 3	6000		1	7	5	6				9			11		10		3	2	4	8
21		20	Lincoln City	0-1		4000		1	7	5	6				9			11		10		3	2	4	8
22		27	LINCOLN CITY	2-1	McCulloch, Eddleston			1		5	6				9	7		11		10		3	2	4	8
23	Feb 3		Durham City	1-0	Eddleston	3000		1		5	6				9	7		11		10		3	2	4	8
24		10	DURHAM CITY	4-0	Hoad, Eddleston 2, Hutchinson	5000		1	10	5					9	7		11			6	3	2	4	8
25		17	Wigan Borough	1-3	Black	15000		1	10	5					9	7		11			6	3	2	4	8
26		24	WIGAN BOROUGH	1-0	Crawshaw	10000		1	9	5	6	10				7		11				3	2	4	8
27	Mar 3		Chesterfield	2-1	Black, Wolstenholme	14280		1	9	5	6	10				7		11				3	2	4	8
28		10	CHESTERFIELD	4-0	Black 2, Braidwood, Crawshaw	12000		1	9	5	6	10				7		11				3	2	4	8
29		17	CREWE ALEXANDRA	0-0		10000		1	9	5	6	10				7		11				3	2	4	8
30		24	Crewe Alexandra	0-1		7000		1		5	6	10			9	7		11				3	2	4	8
31		31	GRIMSBY TOWN	1-1	Eddleston	8000		1		5	6	10			9	7		11				3	2	4	8
32	Apr 2		Wrexham	1-2	Crawshaw	10000		1		5	6	10	2		9	7		11	8			3	4		
33		7	Grimsby Town	2-0	Wolstenholme, Braidwood	6000		1	4	5	6	10			9	7		11				3	2		8
34		14	ACCRINGTON STANLEY	2-1	Crawshaw, Broadhead	8000		1	7	5	6	10			9			11				3	2	4	8
35		21	Accrington Stanley	1-0	Braidwood	10000		1	2	5	6	10			9	7		11	4			3			8
36		24	WREXHAM	2-0	Crawshaw, Eddleston	12000		1	2	5	6	10			9	7		11	4			3			8
37		28	WALSALL	3-0	Eddleston, Wolstenholme 2	7000	1			7	5	6	10	2	9			11	4			3			8
38	May 5		Walsall	0-5		2500	1			2	5	6	10		9	7		11	4			3			8

	Apps	2	1	36	23	38	36	13	2	34	25	1	38	10	28	4	37	24	30	36
	Goals				5	6	1	5		22	1		1		6					13

One own goal

F.A. Cup

Q4	Nov 18	Rochdale	1-0	Eddleston		10000		1	7	5	6				9			11		10		3	2	4	8
Q5	Dec 2	Stalybridge Celtic	0-1			6000		1	7	5	6				9			11		10		3	2	4	8

76

1923-24

21st in Division Two: Relegated

#	Date	Opponent	Score	Scorers	Att	Abbott H	Birds J	Black JR	Braidwood E	Broadhead JE	Cameron ES	Caulfield W	Chadwick E	Collins LR	Crawshaw RL	Eddleston J	Higginbotham H	Hoad SJ	Humphrey D	Hutchinson R	Kennedy S	Lammus WCJ	Lilley R	Lilley T	McCulloch MJ	Newnes J	Nutter H	Rigg C	Thomson J	Ward E	Wilson D	Wolstenholme AE
1	Aug 25	CLAPTON ORIENT	1-1	McCulloch	12000	1	7	5	6							9				11					10		3				4	8
2	27	Stockport County	0-1		11000	1	7	5	6							9				11		2			10		3				4	8
3	Sep 1	Clapton Orient	1-5	Eddleston	20000	1		5	6							9		7		11		2			10		3				4	
4	3	STOCKPORT COUNTY	1-1	Wolstenholme	10000			5	6							9				11		2			4		3					10
5	8	Hull City	1-2	Eddleston	9000	1	7	5						6		9				11		2			4		3					10
6	11	SOUTHAMPTON	0-0		12000	1	7							6		9				11		2			4	5	3				8	10
7	15	HULL CITY	1-1	Eddleston	11000	1		8						7	6	9				11		2			4	5	3		10			8
8	22	Stoke	0-4		14000	1								6	10	9		7		11		2			4	5	3					8
9	29	STOKE	2-0	Newnes (p), Eddleston	10000	1			6					3	10	9		7		11		2			4	5						
10	Oct 6	Crystal Palace	1-1	Roseboom	10000	1			6					3	10	9		7		11					4	5			2			
11	13	CRYSTAL PALACE	4-2	Crawshaw 3, Hoad	10000	1								6	10	9		7		11					4	5	3		2			
12	20	SHEFFIELD WEDNESDAY	1-1	Crawshaw		1								6	10	9		7		11					4	5	3		2			
13	27	Sheffield Wednesday	0-5		16000	1				11				6	10	9		7							4	5	3		2			
14	Nov 3	COVENTRY CITY	3-0	Caulfield 2, Eddleston	6000	1			6		8				10	9		7		11					4	5	3		2			
15	10	Coventry City	0-4		12000	1			6		8	7			10	9				11			2		4	5	3					
16	17	Bristol City	0-1		8000	1		5	6		8					9		7		11					10	4	3		2			
17	24	BRISTOL CITY	2-1	Eddleston 2	8000	1		5	6						10	9		7		11					4		3		2			
18	Dec 8	Southampton	0-3		11000	1		5						6	10	9		7		11					4		3		2			
19	15	Fulham	0-0		13000	1		5	6							9		7		11					10	4	3		2	8		
20	22	FULHAM	1-1	Braidwood	6000	1		5	6							9		7		11					10	4	3		2	8		
21	25	DERBY COUNTY	2-1	Newnes (p), Hoad	10000	1		5						6	10	9		7		11					4		3		2	8		
22	26	Derby County	0-6		16000	1		5						6	10	9		7		11					4		3		2	8		
23	29	Blackpool	1-1	Eddleston	15000	1		5	6		7				10	9									4		3		2	8		
24	Jan 5	BLACKPOOL	2-3	Caulfield, Wolstenholme	10000	1		5	6		7				10	9									4		3		2	8		
25	19	OLDHAM ATHLETIC	2-1	Newnes, Eddleston	9000	1		5	6		8					11	9	7							3	4			2			10
26	26	Oldham Athletic	0-1		12000	1		5	6		8					9		7		11					3	4			2			10
27	Feb 2	SOUTH SHIELDS	0-2		7000	1			6		8					9		7	11		5				3	4			2			10
28	9	South Shields	0-3		8000			5						6		8		7	11		9		2			4	1	3				
29	16	BURY	0-5		8500			5								8		7	11		9		2	6		4	1	3				8
30	23	Bury	0-2		8000	1		5	6						10	9	8	7	11				2			4		3				
31	Mar 1	MANCHESTER UNITED	0-2		7000	1		5	6		7				10	9	8		11				2			4		3				
32	8	Manchester United	1-0	Crawshaw	18000	1		5			7				10	9	8		11				2			4				6		
33	15	Barnsley	0-0		8000			5			11	7				9							2			4		3	1	8	6	10
34	22	BARNSLEY	4-3	Caulfield 2(1p), Eddleston, Hoad	7000			5			11	8				9		7					2			4		3	1		6	10
35	29	Bradford City	2-0	Cameron, Eddleston	10000	1		5			11	7				9					4		2		10			3			6	8
36	Apr 5	BRADFORD CITY	1-1	Cameron	8000	1		5			11	7				9					4		2		10			3			6	8
37	12	PORT VALE	1-3	Cameron	7000	1		5			11	7				9	8				4		2		10			3			6	10
38	19	Port Vale	0-0		8000	1		5			11	8				9		7					2			4		3			6	10
39	21	LEICESTER CITY	1-1	Eddleston	10000	1		5			11	8				9		7					2			4		3			6	10
40	22	Leicester City	1-3	McCulloch	14000	1		5	6							9		7	11				2		10	4		3			6	8
41	26	Leeds United	0-1		20000	1		5								9		7	11				2		10	4		3			6	8
42	May 3	LEEDS UNITED	3-1	Eddleston 2, Chadwick	10000	1		5			11	7	8			9							2			4		3			6	10

JH Steel played in game 1 at 2
EF Gillibrand played in games 23 and 24 at 11
E Roseboom played in games 28 and 29 at 10

Apps	34	4	6	31	21	8	18	3	13	19	40	4	26	8	22	6	8	5	14	21	37	2	37	2	2	31	25
Goals				1		3	5	1		5	14		3						2	3							2

F.A. Cup

	Date	Opponent	Score	Scorers	Att																										
Q5	Dec 1	Wigan Borough	1-1	Ward (og)	12650	1		5						6	10	9		7		11					4		3		2			
rep	5	WIGAN BOROUGH	0-1		4000	1		5						6	10	9		7		11					4		3		2			

1924-25

Second in Division Three (North)

#	Date	Opponent	Score	Scorers	Att	Abbott H	Bottrill WG	Braidwood E	Broadhead JE	Butterworth H	Cameron ES	Chadwick E	Eddleston J	Ellerington W	Harper W	Harris A	Hoad SJ	Laycock FW	Lilley R	Moore W	Newnes J	O'Beirne J	Phizacklea JR	Rigg C	Smith F	Stevenson JA	Wolstenholme AE
1	Aug 30	Southport	0-1		8000	1	8	6			11		9	5			7		2		4	10		3			
2	Sep 6	ASHINGTON	4-0	Eddleston, Hoad, Bottrill, Newnes	6000	1	8	6			11		9	5			7				4	10	2	3			
3	9	DONCASTER ROVERS	3-0	Eddleston 2, Bottrill	5000	1	8	6			11		9	5			7				4	10	2	3			
4	13	Accrington Stanley	0-2		9000	1	8	6			11		9	5			7				4	10	2	3			
5	16	DURHAM CITY	7-1	Eddleston 3,Cameron,Newnes(p),Bottrill,O'Beirne	5000	1	8	6			11		9	5			7				4	10	2	3			
6	20	Barrow	0-3		8000	1	8	6			11		9	5			7				4	10	2	3			
7	27	LINCOLN CITY	1-0	O'Beirne	7000	1	8	6			11		9	5			7				4	10	2	3			
8	Oct 4	Tranmere Rovers	0-2		7000	1	8	6			11		9	5			7				4	10	2	3			
9	11	WALSALL	2-1	Eddleston 2	7000	1	8	6			11		9	5			7		2		4	10	3				
10	18	Wigan Borough	1-1	Eddleston	15000	1	8	6			11	10	9	5			7		2		4		3				
11	25	HALIFAX TOWN	2-1	Cameron, Braidwood	10000	1	10	6			11	8	9	5					2	7	4		3				
12	Nov 1	New Brighton	0-5		4000	1	8	6			11		9	5					2	7	4	10	3				
13	8	GRIMSBY TOWN	1-0	Bottrill	6000	1	8	6			11		9	5			7				4		2	3			10
14	15	Darlington	1-3	Wolstenholme	7000	1	8	6			11		9	5			7				4		2	3			10
15	22	ROCHDALE	1-0	Bottrill	5000	1	8	6					9	5			7				4	11	2	3			10
16	Dec 6	BRADFORD PARK AVE.	2-2	Eddleston, Rigg (p)	6000	1	8	6			11		9	5			7				4		2	3			10
17	20	ROTHERHAM COUNTY	4-1	Eddleston 2, Bottrill, Chadwick	4000	1	8	5				10	9	6			7				4	11	2	3			
18	25	CHESTERFIELD	1-0	Ellerington	6000	1		6			11		9	5	4		7					10	2	3			8
19	26	Chesterfield	1-0	Wolstenholme	9000	1		6			11		9	5			7				4	10	2	3			8
20	Jan 3	Ashington	1-1	Ellerington	4245	1	8	6			11		9	5			7				4	10	2	3			
21	10	Wrexham	1-1	Braidwood	5000	1	8	6			11	10	9	5			7		2		4			3			
22	17	ACCRINGTON STANLEY	4-1	Eddleston 2, Chadwick, Cameron	6000	1	8	6			11	10	9	5			7		2		4			3			
23	24	BARROW	2-0	Rigg 2 (2p)	5000	1	8	6			11	10	9	5			7		2		4			3			
24	Feb 7	TRANMERE ROVERS	4-1	Rigg (p), Chadwick 2, Cameron	4000	1	7	5		6	11	10	9						2		4			3			8
25	14	Walsall	2-1	Hoad, Chadwick	4000	1	8	5		6	11	10	9				7		2		4			3			
26	21	WIGAN BOROUGH	1-0	Braidwood	6000	1	8	5		6	11	10	9				7		2		4			3			
27	28	Halifax Town	4-2	Chadwick, Cameron, Eddleston, Bottrill	10000	1	8	5		6	11	10	9				7		2		4			3			
28	Mar 7	NEW BRIGHTON	5-0	Bottrill, Eddleston 2, Hoad, Chadwick	6000	1	8	5		6	11	10	9				7		2		4			3			
29	14	Grimsby Town	0-2		5000	1	8	5		6		10	9				7		2		4	11		3			
30	18	Lincoln City	1-2	Stevenson			1		5		6	11	10	9		2		7				4			3		8	
31	21	HARTLEPOOLS UNITED	2-0	Chadwick, Eddleston	6000	1		5			11	10	9			6	7	4			2			3		8	
32	25	Hartlepools United	4-2	Eddleston 3, Cameron	1500	1		5			11		9			2	6	7	8				O'Beirne	3		10	
33	28	Rochdale	1-0	Laycock	8000	1		5			11		9			2	6	7	8		4			3		10	
34	Apr 4	DARLINGTON	1-1	Eddleston	13500	1		5			11		9			2	6	7	8		4			3		10	
35	10	Crewe Alexandra	1-2	Newnes	7000	1		5			11	10	9				6		8	2	4			3		7	
36	11	Bradford Park Avenue	1-1	Stevenson	10000	1		5			11	10	9	6					8	2	4			3		7	
37	13	CREWE ALEXANDRA	7-0	Eddleston 3, Laycock 2, Cameron, Chadwick	6000	1		5			11	10	9	6					8	2	4			3		7	
38	14	Doncaster Rovers	1-1	Stevenson	4000	1		5			11	10	9	6	2				8		4			3		7	
39	18	WREXHAM	2-4	Laycock 2	5000	1		5			11	10	9		2	6			8		4			3		7	
40	21	SOUTHPORT	2-1	Laycock 2	6000	1		5	6		11		9						8	2	4			3	10	7	
41	25	Rotherham County	0-1		4000	1	7	5	6		11		9						8	2	4			3		10	
42	29	Durham City	1-3	Chadwick	2000	1	7	5	6			10				4		9	2					3		8	

A Bottrill played in game 42 at 11

Apps	42	29	42	3	7	38	20	41	26	6	8	31	12	17	5	40	16	19	38	1	13	7		
Goals		8	3			7	10	25	2			3	7			3	2		4		3	2		

F.A. Cup

	Date	Opponent	Score	Scorers	Att																						
Q5	Nov 29	WINSFORD UNITED	4-1	* see below	4000	1	8	6					9	5			7				4	11	2	3			10
Q6	Dec 13	COVENTRY CITY	0-1		7000	1	8	6			11		9	5			7				4	10	2	3			

Scorers in Q5: Wolstenholme, Braidwood, Eddleston, O'Beirne

1925-26

8th in Division Three (North)

#	Date		Opponent	Score	Scorers	Att	Abbott H	Bailey F	Bottrill WG	Braidwood E	Broadhead JE	Broadhurst F	Butterworth H	Chadwick E	Chadwick W	Clayton H	Cowen JE	Denwood W	Earle EJ	Eddleston J	Hampson J	Harris A	Hoad SJ	Laycock FW	Mace F	Newnes J	Pearson JS	Rigg C	Smith F	Stevenson JA	Wilson G
1	Aug 29		CREWE ALEXANDRA	2-1	Eddleston, Bottrill	10112	1		8	4	6	2					11			9			7					3		10	5
2		31	Ashington	1-5	Stevenson	3902	1		8	4	6						11						7	9		2		3		10	5
3	Sep	5	Lincoln City	0-1		7774	1			4	6	2					11			9			7	8				3		10	5
4		8	BARROW	3-3	Laycock, Hoad, Eddleston	6522	1			4	6	2		10						9				8				3		11	5
5		12	SOUTHPORT	3-3	Stevenson, Wilson, Hampson	6718	1			4	6	2		10									7	9				3		11	5
6		15	ASHINGTON	2-2	Eddleston, Hampson	7461	1				6	2							11	9	8		7					4		3	10	5
7		19	Doncaster Rovers	1-1	Bottrill	3088	1		7		6	2		10					11	9	8							4		3		5
8		26	WREXHAM	5-1	Laycock,Bottrill,Chadwick 2,Eddleston	6669	1		7		6	2		10					11	9				8				4		3		5
9		28	Barrow	0-1		1601	1		7		6	2		10					11	9				8				4		3		5
10	Oct	3	Coventry City	0-1		11766	1		8		6	2		10					11	9			7					4	3			5
11		10	ACCRINGTON STANLEY	1-0	Chadwick	9119	1		8		6	2		10					11				7					4	3		9	5
12		17	Durham City	2-0	Chadwick	3538	1		8		6	2		10					11	9			7					4	3			5
13		24	HARTLEPOOLS UNITED	5-2	Wilson (p), Chadwick 3, Eddleston	4892	1		8		6	2		10					11	9			7					4	3			5
14		31	Rotherham United	3-1	Bottrill, Eddleston 2	7360	1		8		6	2		10					11	9			7					4	3			5
15	Nov	7	HALIFAX TOWN	1-1	Wilson (p)	4538	1		8		6	2		10					11	9			7					4	3			5
16		14	Walsall	2-0	Chadwick, Eddleston	2586	1		8		6	2		10					11				7					4	3			5
17	Dec	5	GRIMSBY TOWN	1-1	Cowen	5675	1		8			2					9		11		10	6	7					4	3			5
18		12	Halifax Town	1-1	Bottrill	7204	1		8			2		10					11	9		6	7					4	3			5
19		19	TRANMERE ROVERS	7-0	Hampson 3, Earle, Hoad 2, Stevenson	4354	1		8			2							11		9	6	7					4	3		10	5
20		25	WIGAN BOROUGH	7-0	Bottrill,Hampson 3,Earle 2,Stevenson	7658	1		8			2							11		9	6	7					4	3		10	5
21		26	New Brighton	0-0		6973	1		8			2							11		9	6	7					4	3		10	5
22	Jan	2	Crewe Alexandra	4-1	Hampson 3, Earle	6387	1		8			2							11		9	6	7					4	3		10	5
23		9	Bradford Park Avenue	0-3		20946	1		8			2							11		9	6	7					4	3		10	5
24		16	LINCOLN CITY	5-2	Bottrill 2, Cowen 2, Newnes	5586	1		8			2					9		11			6	7			4			3		10	5
25		23	Southport	1-2	Cowen	4214	1		8			2				3	9		11			6	7					4			10	5
26		30	DONCASTER ROVERS	5-3	Eddleston 3, Bottrill 2	6402	1		8			2							11	9		6	7					4	3		10	5
27	Feb	6	Wrexham	2-3	Eddleston, Bottrill	4792	1		8	6		2							11	9			7					4	3		10	5
28		13	COVENTRY CITY	4-1	Eddleston, Stevenson, Hoad, Earle	6250	1		8			2	6		4				11	9			7						3		10	5
29		20	Accrington Stanley	2-3	Bottrill, Eddleston	7153	1		8			2			6				11	9			7					4	3		10	5
30		27	DURHAM CITY	4-0	Earle, Bottrill 2, Wilson (p)	4819	1		8			2			4				11	9		6	7						3		10	5
31	Mar	6	Hartlepools United	0-2		4397	1		8			2							11	9		4	7			6			3		10	5
32		13	ROTHERHAM UNITED	3-0	Bottrill 2, Stevenson	4451	1		8			2							11	7	9	6						4	3		10	5
33		23	Rochdale	0-2		2981	1		8			2							11	7	9	6						4	3		10	5
34		27	WALSALL	2-0	Eddleston 2	4786	1		7			2							11	9	8	6						4	3		10	5
35	Apr	3	Chesterfield	1-3	Eddleston	8743	1		7			2							11	9	8	6						4	3		10	5
36		5	NEW BRIGHTON	1-1	Wilson	5858	1		7			2	6						11	9	8							4	3		10	5
37		6	Wigan Borough	0-5		4198	1		8			2							11	7	9							4	3		10	5
38		10	BRADFORD PARK AVE.	2-2	Earle, Laycock (p)	14143	1		8			2							11	9	10	6		7				4	3			5
39		17	Grimsby Town	0-3		9641	1		7					2					11	9	10	6		8				4	3			5
40		20	CHESTERFIELD	3-3	Laycock 2 (1p), Hampson	3989	1		7					2					11	9	10	6		8	1		4		3			5
41		24	ROCHDALE	1-3	Eddleston	6215	1		7			2							11	10	9	6		8				4	3			5
42	May	1	Tranmere Rovers	2-4	Hampson, Eddleston	2884	1	4	7										11	10	9	6		8				2	3			5
			Apps				41	1	38	17	6	37	2	13	2	4	3	3	37	31	20	22	28	11	1	36	8	33	1	25	42
			Goals						16					8			4		7	20	13		4	5		1				6	5

F.A. Cup

| R1 | Dec | 2 | Wigan Borough | 0-3 | | 3836 | 1 | | 8 | 6 | | 2 | | 10 | | | | | 11 | 9 | | | 7 | | | | | 4 | 3 | | | 5 |

79

1926-27

5th in Division Three (North)

#	Date	Opponent	Score	Scorers	Att	Abbott H	Bailey F	Baker JW	Bedford L	Bottrill WG	Broadhurst F	Brown J	Earle EJ	Hampson J	Harris A	Hoad SJ	Keers JM	Mace F	Mitchell R	Pearson JS	Pickering T	Rigg C	Roberts P	Sharp B	Simpson E	Stevenson JA	Taylor H	White HA	Wilson G
1	Aug 28	Wigan Borough	1-2	Sharp	6788	1		4		8			11	9		7			6	3		2		10					5
2	Sep 4	DONCASTER ROVERS	5-1	Earle 3, Bottrill, Stevenson	6982	1		4		8			11			7			6	3		2		10		9			5
3	11	Stoke City	1-4	Sharp	11199	1		4		8			11			7			6	3		2	9	10					5
4	13	ASHINGTON	4-0	Earle, Sharp 2 (1p), Bottrill	5595	1				8	2		11		4	7			6	3				9		10			5
5	15	NEW BRIGHTON	2-0	Sharp 2	5244	1				9	2		11		4	7			6	3				10		8			5
6	18	ROTHERHAM UNITED	5-3	Baker 2 (2p), Bottrill, Sharp, Stevenson	6395	1		5		9	2		11		4	7			6	3				10		8			
7	25	Bradford Park Avenue	2-2	Earle, Bottrill	11992	1		6		7	2		11		4				9	3				10		8			5
8	Oct 2	WALSALL	3-2	Sharp, Stevenson, Earle	6295	1		4		7			11	9					6	3		2		10		8			5
9	9	Lincoln City	4-1	Harris, Stevenson, Hampson, Earle	4920	1		4		7			11	9	8				6	3		2				10			5
10	16	DURHAM CITY	1-1	Baker (p)	5517	1		4		7	2		11	9	8				6					3	10		8			5
11	23	Accrington Stanley	5-0	Hoad 2, Stevenson 2, Sharp	6804	1		4					11	9	6	7						2		3	10		8			5
12	30	HALIFAX TOWN	0-0		7316	1		4					11	9	6	7						2		3	10		8			5
13	Nov 6	Barrow	1-0	Stevenson	3526	1		4					11	9	6	7						2		3	10		8			5
14	13	CREWE ALEXANDRA	7-1	Hampson 4, Stevenson, Baker (p), Sharp	4149	1		4		7			11	9					6	2				3	10		8			5
15	20	Hartlepools United	2-3	Sharp, Hampson	3171	1		4		7			11	9					6	2				3	10		8			5
16	Dec 4	Southport	4-3	Hampson 2, Wilson, Earle	4438	1		4		7			11	9					6	2				3	10		8			5
17	18	Tranmere Rovers	3-2	Hampson, Stevenson, Sharp	3970	1					2		11	9	6	7								3	10		8			5
18	27	Wrexham	2-2	Sharp 2	10362	1		4			2			9	6	7								3	10		8	11		5
19	Jan 1	WREXHAM	3-0	Stevenson 2, Sharp	6485	1		4			2					7	11		6				9	3	10		8			5
20	8	STOCKPORT COUNTY	6-1	Hampson 3, Keers, Sharp 2	4129	1		4			2			9		7	11		6					3	10		8			5
21	15	WIGAN BOROUGH	4-0	Baker, Sharp, Keers, Hampson	5205	1		5			2			9	4	7	11		6					3	10		8			5
22	22	Doncaster Rovers	0-6		4977	1		4			2			9		7	11		6					3	10		8			5
23	29	STOKE CITY	1-0	Sharp	9974	1		4			2			9		7	11		6	3					10		8			5
24	Feb 5	Rotherham United	3-2	Sharp, Hampson, Keers	4345	1		4		7	2			9			11		6					3	10		8			5
25	12	BRADFORD PARK AVE.	1-0	Baker	12415	1		4	8	2		7		9			11		6					3	10					5
26	19	Walsall	1-4	Sharp	3498	1		4			2	7		9			11		6					3	10		8			5
27	26	LINCOLN CITY	2-1	Stevenson, Sharp	5784	1		4		7	2			9					6					3	10		8	11		5
28	Mar 5	Durham City	2-1	Hampson 2, Sharp	1135	1		4		7	2			9					6					3	10		8	11		5
29	12	ACCRINGTON STANLEY	7-0	Hampson 3, Bedford 2, Wilson, White	7046	1		4	11	7	2			9					6					3	10				8	5
30	19	Halifax Town	1-4	White	13602	1		4	11	7	2			9					6					3	10				8	5
31	23	Ashington	1-1	White	1047	1				11				9	4	7			6	2				3	10				8	5
32	26	BARROW	3-0	Hampson, White, Bedford	3668	1				11				9		7			4	2				3			6		10	8	5
33	Apr 2	Crewe Alexandra	1-2	Stevenson	5225	1				11				9	4	7			6	2				3			10		8	5
34	5	ROCHDALE	3-1	Hampson 2, White	5871	1				11				9	4	7			6	2				3			10		8	5
35	9	HARTLEPOOLS UNITED	6-2	White 3, Hampson, Stevenson, Wilson	4369					11				9	4	7		1	6	2				3			10		8	5
36	15	Chesterfield	1-1	Bedford	12744					11				9	4	7		1	6	2				3			10		8	5
37	16	Stockport County	1-4	Wilson	10546					7				9	4			1	6	2				3			10	11	8	5
38	18	CHESTERFIELD	0-3		6699					7	2			9	4			1						3	10	6		11	8	5
39	23	SOUTHPORT	1-2	Stevenson	3473					11				9	4	7		1						3	6		10		8	5
40	27	New Brighton	2-7	Stevenson 2	3104		4			11				9		7		1						3	10	6	8			5
41	30	Rochdale	1-2	Wilson	3871	1	4			11				9		7								3	6		8		10	5
42	May 7	TRANMERE ROVERS	0-2		2385		4			11				9		7		1						3	6		8		10	5

	Apps	Goals
Abbott H	35	
Bailey F	3	
Baker JW	28	6
Bedford L	14	4
Bottrill WG	19	4
Broadhurst F	24	
Brown J	2	
Earle EJ	17	8
Hampson J	35	23
Harris A	20	1
Hoad SJ	26	2
Keers JM	8	3
Mace F	7	
Mitchell R	32	
Pearson JS	23	
Pickering T	1	
Rigg C	37	
Roberts P	1	
Sharp B	35	23
Simpson E	2	
Stevenson JA	35	17
Taylor H	5	
White HA	13	8
Wilson G	40	5

F.A. Cup

#	Date	Opponent	Score	Scorers	Att	Abbott H	Baker JW	Bottrill WG	Earle EJ	Hampson J	Mitchell R	Pearson JS	Rigg C	Sharp B	Stevenson JA	Wilson G
R1	Nov 27	STOCKPORT COUNTY	4-1	Hampson 2, Sharp, Stevenson	8757	1	4	7		11	9	6	2	3	10	8	5
R2	Dec 11	Ashington	1-2	Stevenson	5265	1	4	7	2	11	9	6		3	10	8	5

1927-28

22nd in Division Three (North)

#	Date	Opponent	Score	Scorers	Att	Bedford L	Bossons WH	Bottrill WG	Cochrane DS	Fletcher J	Halliwell JA	Hampson J	Harris A	Hayes GT	Hepworth A	Jones JW	McClure D	McGuire J	Pearson JS	Radford B	Ridge D	Rigg C	Ruffell WG	Sharp B	Simpson E	Slack WB	Spence GB	Stoneham J	Taylor H	Warhurst SL	White HA	Wilson G
1	Aug 27	ACCRINGTON STANLEY	1-4	Sharp	8007	11		7			4	9			3							2		10	6			1			8	5
2	Sep 3	Rochdale	0-1		9869	11		7			4	9			3							2		10	6			1			8	5
3	10	ROTHERHAM UNITED	6-1	Hampson 2,Bottrill,White 2,Sharp	4881	11		7			4	9			3							2		10	6			1			8	5
4	12	BARROW	4-0	Bedford, White 2, Bottrill	4928	11		7			4	9			3							2		10	6			1			8	5
5	17	Southport	2-1	Hampson, Bedford	5406	11		7			5	9	4		3							2	8	10	6			1				5
6	24	DURHAM CITY	2-1	Hampson 2	5495	11		7			4	9					3					2	10	8						1		5
7	29	Barrow	1-3	Bedford	4306	11		7			4	9					3					2		10						1	8	5
8	Oct 1	Wrexham	2-5	White 2	4828	11					4	9	6				3					2	7	10						1	8	5
9	8	CHESTERFIELD	3-3	Hampson, White (p), Sharp	4659	11	1				4	9	6				3					2		10		7					8	5
10	15	Bradford Park Avenue	2-3	Sharp, Bottrill	14833	11		8			2		4									3		10		7				1	9	6
11	22	NEW BRIGHTON	0-3		2698	11		8			4						3					2	10		6	7				1	9	5
12	29	Lincoln City	0-0		7956	11		8		9	4						3	2						10	6	7				1		5
13	Nov 5	HARTLEPOOLS UNITED	4-2	Sharp 3, Spence	2001	11		8			4						3					2	10	9	6	7				1		5
14	12	Bradford City	1-9	Cochrane	15638	11		8	9	*	4				3							2		10	6	7	1					5
15	19	HALIFAX TOWN	3-2	Bottrill, Cochrane, Sharp	3862		1	8	9	11	4				3			2						10	6	7						5
16	Dec 3	ASHINGTON	1-5	Spence	2936		1	8		11	10				3		9	2		4					6	7						5
17	10	Wigan Borough	2-4	Ruffell, McGuire	2736		1	8			4				3	2	9						7	10	6					11		5
18	17	DONCASTER ROVERS	0-1		3410	11		8			4					2	9			10		3	7	6					1		5
19	27	Tranmere Rovers	1-1	Bedford	8946	11		7			4					2	9			10		3	8	6					1		5
20	31	Accrington Stanley	1-7	Ruffell	4207	11		7			4					2	9			10		3	8	6					1		5
21	Jan 2	Crewe Alexandra	1-6	Wilson (p)	2430	11		7			4		6		3		9					2					10	1				5
22	7	ROCHDALE	6-3	* see below	2539			8			4					2	10		9	6	3					7			11	1		5
23	14	Halifax Town	1-5	Radford	3119			7			4					2			9	6	3	10				8			11	1		5
24	21	Rotherham United	3-4	Sharp, Taylor 2	4505			7			4					2	10	3	9				6						11	1		5
25	Feb 4	Durham City	0-3		1537			7			4					2	10		9				6						11	1		5
26	11	WREXHAM	4-0	Radford 4 (1p)	2721			7			4					2	10		9		3		6						11	1		5
27	18	Chesterfield	0-6		3804			7			4					2	10		9		3		8	6					11	1		5
28	25	BRADFORD PARK AVE.	1-2	Wilson (p)	8096			7			4		6			2	10		9		3		8						11	1		5
29	Mar 3	New Brighton	0-4		4290			7			4					2	6		9		3		10						11	1		5
30	10	LINCOLN CITY	1-3	Bottrill	3422			8		11	4		6			2			9		3	7	10						1			5
31	17	Hartlepools United	5-4	Sharp,Slack,Radford 2,Bottrill	2972			7			4			8	6	2			9		3		10		11							5
32	20	SOUTHPORT	1-1	Bottrill	3583			7			4			10	6	2			9		3		8		11							5
33	24	BRADFORD CITY	0-3		5085			7			4			10	6	2	3		9				8		11				1			5
34	Apr 6	Stockport County	0-8		8430			7			4					2	6	8	9	3			10		11				1			5
35	7	DARLINGTON	4-0	Sharp, Taylor, Hayes 2 (1p)	3816						4			9	6	2	8	3					10					7	11	1		5
36	9	STOCKPORT COUNTY	0-4		5441						4			9	6	2	8	3					10					7	11	1		5
37	14	Ashington	1-5	Slack	1410						2			9	6					4	3		8	10	11	7				1			5
38	16	Darlington	1-4	Hayes	1003			7			2		4	8	6							5	3	10	9	11				1			5
39	21	CREWE ALEXANDRA	3-3	Slack, Radford, Sharp	2349						4				6	2	7			9	5	3		10	11					1			5
40	24	TRANMERE ROVERS	3-5	Hayes, Radford 2	1126						6			8		2	7			9	4	3		10	11					1			5
41	28	Doncaster Rovers	2-4	Radford, Hayes	4117			7			4			9						8		10	5	2		6		11		1			3
42	May 5	WIGAN BOROUGH	2-4	Radford 2, Wilson	2183			7			4				6	2	8			9		3		10	11					1			5

Scorers in game 22: Radford 3, Taylor, McClure, McGuire
Played in one game: JE Broadhurst (10, at 5), A Jones (25, at 3),
J Mangham (31, in goal).

	Apps	18	4	35	2	4	42	9	8	9	10	12	28	20	7	20	8	32	12	37	15	10	13	6	12	31	9	39
	Goals	3		7	2		6	5				1	2		17			3	11	3	2		4		7	3	

A Brown played in games 6 and 7 at 6.
J Dargon played in games 24 and 39 at 8.
RH Gaskell played in three games, 25, 26 and 29, at 8.

F.A. Cup

| R1 | Nov 26 | BRADFORD PARK AVE. | 0-3 | | 9000 | | 1 | 8 | 9 | 11 | 4 | | | | 3 | | | 2 | | | | | 10 | | | 7 | 6 | | | | | 5 |

81

1928-29

15th in Division Three (North)

#	Date	Opponent	Score	Scorers	Att	Brooks J	Buchanan J	Carmedy TO	Dodsworth JG	Donkin W	Fawcett DH	Ferguson E	Fletcher J	Gilan F	Halliwell JA	Hepworth A	Hooper A	Hooper HR	Kelly GM	McDonagh P	Metcalfe JA	Morton W	Radford B	Ridley H	Rigg C	Sharp B	Suttie D	Tordoff H	Warhurst SL	Wilkinson T	Wilson G
1	Aug 25	Hartlepools United	2-2	Ridley, Radford	5524					2	1				6		3		7		4		9	11		8				10	5
2	Sep 1	DARLINGTON	2-1	Sharp, Wilkinson	7337					2	1				6		3		7		4		9	11		8				10	5
3	8	Southport	1-5	Kelly	4188					2	1				6		3		7	8	4		9	11		5				10	
4	12	SOUTH SHIELDS	1-0	Kelly	5843						1	2			6		3		7		4		9	11		8				10	5
5	15	ROCHDALE	3-0	Wilson (p), Wilkinson, Radford	6715						1	2			6		3		7	8	4		9	11						10	5
6	22	New Brighton	1-0	Radford	4882						1	2			6		3		7		4		9	11		8				10	5
7	25	LINCOLN CITY	3-4	Radford 2, Wilkinson	4970						1	2			6		3		7		5		9	11		8	4			10	
8	29	WREXHAM	1-3	Ridley	6280						1				6		3		7		5		9	11		8	4			10	
9	Oct 2	DONCASTER ROVERS	2-4	Radford, Suttie	3297					2	1	3			6				7	8	5		9	10			4			11	
10	6	Chesterfield	2-3	Kelly 2	5247					2	1	3	5						7	8	6		9	11		10	4				
11	13	BARROW	3-4	Radford 2, Wilson (p)	4616		8			2	1	3	4						7	10	6		9	11							5
12	20	Carlisle United	0-4		2321		8			2	1				6			3	7		4		9	11						10	5
13	27	ROTHERHAM UNITED	4-2	Radford, Buchanan, Wilkinson, Kelly	3795		8				1								2	7	4		9	11	3		6			10	5
14	Nov 3	Wigan Borough	0-1		6928		8			2									7		4		9	11	3		6		1	10	5
15	10	CREWE ALEXANDRA	4-1	Radford 2, Wilson (p), Ridley	7445		8			2									7		4		9	11	3		6		1	10	5
16	17	Tranmere Rovers	1-6	Radford	4393		8			2									7		4		9	11	3		6		1	10	5
17	Dec 1	Halifax Town	2-1	Suttie, Halliwell	5988		8			2			5	9					7		4		10	11	3		6		1		
18	8	ASHINGTON	5-0	Kelly 2, Radford 2, Wilkinson	2915		8			2			5	9					7		4		10		3		6		1	11	
19	15	Bradford City	2-0	Halliwell, Buchanan	13236		8			2			5	9					7		4		10		3		6		1	11	
20	22	ACCRINGTON STANLEY	0-2		4791		8			2			5	9					7		4		10		3		6		1	11	
21	26	Doncaster Rovers	2-2	Halliwell, Kelly	7369		8			2			5	9					7		4		10	11	3		6		1		
22	29	HARTLEPOOLS UNITED	1-0	Halliwell	3507		8			2			5	9	3				7		4		10	11			6		1		
23	Jan 1	Ashington	2-3	Radford, Ridley	1344		8						5	9					7		4		10	11			6		1		3
24	5	Darlington	2-3	Radford 2	3273		8						2	11	9			3	7		4		10				6		1		5
25	19	SOUTHPORT	1-1	Carmedy	3035		8	9					2	11				3	7		4						6		1		5
26	22	STOCKPORT COUNTY	4-1	Morton 2, Ridley, Kelly (p)	2749		8						2		10	6		3	7		4	9		11					1		5
27	26	Rochdale	1-2	Halliwell	4902		8						2		10	6		3	7		4	9		11					1		5
28	Feb 2	NEW BRIGHTON	3-0	Kelly 2, Buchanan (p)	3168		8		4				2		10	6		3	7		5	9		11					1		
29	9	Wrexham	1-3	Halliwell	5534		8		4				2		10	6		3	7		5	9		11					1		
30	16	CHESTERFIELD	1-0	Radford	2943		8	11			1	2		5	9	6		3	7		4		10								
31	23	Barrow	2-7	Radford 2	5368		8	11					2		5	10	6		3	7		4		9					1		
32	Mar 2	CARLISLE UNITED	1-0	Ridley	4107		8	7					2			10		3			4		9	11		6			1		5
33	9	Rotherham United	0-4		3939		8						2			10		3	7		4		9	11		6			1		5
34	16	WIGAN BOROUGH	2-1	Radford 2	3903	2	8				1	3			10				7		4		9	11		6					5
35	23	Crewe Alexandra	1-1	Halliwell	2976	2	8	9			1	3			10				7		4			11		6					5
36	30	TRANMERE ROVERS	4-2	Radford 2, Buchanan, Wilson	4245	2	8				1	3	11		10				7		4		9			6					5
37	Apr 1	South Shields	2-3	Buchanan (p), Halliwell	4334	2	8				1	3	11		10				7		4		9			6					5
38	6	Stockport County	0-3		7916	3	8				1	2							7		4	10	9	11		6					5
39	13	HALIFAX TOWN	3-1	Fletcher, Morton, Carmedy	3182		8	7			1	2	11			3					4	9	10			6					5
40	20	Lincoln City	1-5	Carmedy	4036	3	8	9			1	2	11						7		4	10				6					5
41	27	BRADFORD CITY	0-1		14979		8	7			1	2									4	9	10	11	3	6					5
42	May 4	Accrington Stanley	4-4	Wilson, Buchanan, Halliwell, Ridley	2671		8				1	2	7		9								10	11	3	6	4				5
				Apps		6	32	8	2	8	23	36	7	11	32	6	9	13	38	5	41	8	35	31	11	8	28	1	19	17	27
				Goals			6	3					1		9				11		3	24	7		1	2				5	5

F.A. Cup

Did not enter: failed to submit entry by the required date

82

1929-30

19th in Division Three (North)

#	Date	Opponent	Score	Scorers	Att	Baldwin J	Botto LA	Buchanan J	Caine J	Carmedy TO	Chapman R	Dixon E	Fairhurst WS	Ferguson E	Ferguson R	Ferrari FW	Gartside R	Hedley F	Hooper HR	Kelly GM	Mangham J	McKinnell JTB	McLaughlan G	Metcalfe JA	Parry FT	Richmond G	Shevlin P	Spargo S	Suttie D	Tordoff H	Warhurst SL	Weedall JT	Wilson G
1	Aug 31	SOUTHPORT	2-2	Buchanan, R Jones (og)	5434			8					3	2		9		11		7				10	4				6				5
2	Sep 4	Darlington	1-6	Ferrari	5687			8		7			3	2		9		11			1			10	4				6				5
3	7	Crewe Alexandra	0-4		4131	1		8					3		10	9		11	2	7				4					6				5
4	11	DARLINGTON	0-1		4002	8		11		10			3			9		7	2								1	4	6				5
5	14	YORK CITY	3-1	Buchanan 2, Ferrari	4483			8					3			9		11	2	7				10			1	4	6				5
6	21	Stockport County	1-6	Ferrari	7789			8					3			9		11	2	7				10			1	4	6				5
7	24	Accrington Stanley	0-3		7108			8					3	2		9				7				10			1	5	6	4		11	
8	28	NEW BRIGHTON	2-1	Kelly 2	3458			8	9				3	2						7				10	4		1		6			11	5
9	Oct 1	WREXHAM	4-0	Hadley, Carmedy 3	2302			8	9				3	2				11		7				10	4		1		6				5
10	5	Port Vale	1-3	Kelly	7746			8	9				3	2				11		7				10	4		1		6	5			
11	12	BARROW	2-0	Hedley, Buchanan	3732			8	7				3	2			9	11						10	4		1		6	5			
12	19	Hartlepools United	2-1	Dixon, Kelly	5695			8				9	3	2				11		7				10	5		1	6	4				
13	26	DONCASTER ROVERS	4-1	* See below	4324			8	7			9	3	2				11						10	5		1	6	4				
14	Nov 2	Chesterfield	0-3		3956			8	7			9	3	2				11						10	5		1	6	4				
15	9	LINCOLN CITY	0-0		3692			8				9	3	2				11						10	5	7	1	6	4				
16	16	Tranmere Rovers	3-2	Dixon 3	4880			8				9	3	2				11					6	10	5	7	1		4				
17	23	HALIFAX TOWN	1-0	Buchanan (p)	2568			8				9	3	2				11					6	10	5	7	1		4				
18	Dec 14	South Shields	1-2	Buchanan (p)	3361			8				9	3	2				11					6	10	5	7	1		4				
19	21	ACCRINGTON STANLEY	2-1	Carmedy, McLaughlan	3806			4		9		8	3	2				11					6	10	5	7	1						
20	25	CARLISLE UNITED	2-2	Dixon, Parry	3454			4		9		8	3	2				11						10	5	7	1		6				
21	28	Southport	0-0		1825			4		9		8	3	2				11				10			5	7	1		6				
22	Jan 4	CREWE ALEXANDRA	1-1	Hedley	3762					9		8	3	2				11					6	10	5	7	1		4				
23	14	ROCHDALE	1-0	Hedley	1359			8		9			3					11	2			10			5	7	1	4	6				
24	18	York City	0-1		5289			8		9			3					11	2				6	10		7	1	4		5			
25	23	Carlisle United	2-2	Carmedy, Parry	3960					9		8	3	2				11					10	6		7	1	4		5			
26	25	STOCKPORT COUNTY	1-2	Manoch	5217					9		10	3	2				11				8	6			7	1	4		5			
27	Feb 1	New Brighton	1-2	Buchanan	3906			8		9		10	3						2			11	6			7	1		4	5			
28	8	PORT VALE	2-3	Carmedy, Weedall	5045			8		9		10	3						2					4	7		1		6	5		11	
29	15	Barrow	2-0	Weedall, Carmedy (p)	4916					9		10	3	2								8			5	7	1		4			11	6
30	22	HARTLEPOOLS UNITED	3-2	Buchanan, Hedley, Dixon	2862			8				9	3	2				11					6	10	5	7	1		4				6
31	Mar 1	Doncaster Rovers	0-3		4445			8	5			9		2				11					6	10		7	3	1	4				
32	8	CHESTERFIELD	0-2		3077			10	5	7		9		2								8			4	11	3	1	6				
33	15	Lincoln City	1-4	Dixon	2057					11	7	9	3	2								8		10	5		1	6	4				
34	22	TRANMERE ROVERS	0-1		2403					11	7	9	3	2								8		10	5		1	6	4				
35	24	Rotherham United	2-1	Dixon 2	1831			8		7		9	3	2										10	5		1	6	4			11	
36	29	Halifax Town	1-1	Carmedy	4185			8		11		9	3	2								10			5	7	1	6	4				
37	Apr 5	ROTHERHAM UNITED	0-1		2280			4		9		10	3	2								8		11		7	1	5	6				
38	12	Rochdale	1-4	Carmedy	2621			4		11	7	9	3	2										10	8		1	5	6				
39	18	WIGAN BOROUGH	1-3	Carmedy	1795			8		9	7		3	2										10	5	11	1	4	6				
40	19	SOUTH SHIELDS	0-1		1553						7	9	3									8		10	5	11	2	4	6		1		
41	21	Wigan Borough	0-2		3004					8		9	3									10			7	2		4	6		1	11	5
42	May 3	Wrexham	1-5	Weedall	1926			8		9	7	10	3											4	2	1		6			11	5

Scorers in game 13: McLaughlan, Metcalfe, Dixon, Buchanan (p)

	Apps	1	1	34	2	29	6	28	40	31	1	7	1	26	8	9	1	13	10	29	30	24	5	37	21	38	8	3	7	12
	Goals			9		10		10				3		5		4			1	2	1	2					3				

One own goal

F.A. Cup

| R1 | Nov 30 | CREWE ALEXANDRA | 0-3 | | 3000 | | | 8 | | | | | 9 | 3 | 2 | | | 11 | | | | | 6 | 10 | | 7 | 1 | 5 | 4 | | | | |

1930-31

Bottom of Division Three (North): Not re-elected

#	Date	Opponent	Score	Scorers	Att
1	Aug 30	Rochdale	4-5	Bate 3, Carmedy	4822
2	Sep 2	HULL CITY	0-2		5128
3	6	DARLINGTON	3-1	Bate 2, Howarth	3299
4	10	LINCOLN CITY	1-2	Howarth	3955
5	13	Halifax Town	0-1		5433
6	15	Lincoln City	0-2		6741
7	20	NEW BRIGHTON	2-2	H Robinson, Hawes	2585
8	27	Stockport County	0-1		6822
9	Oct 4	GATESHEAD	2-2	Raisbeck 2	2321
10	11	Doncaster Rovers	0-2		3542
11	18	Crewe Alexandra	2-4	H Robinson, Raisbeck	4143
12	25	ACCRINGTON STANLEY	4-2	Raisbeck, Carmedy 3	2756
13	Nov 1	Tranmere Rovers	1-7	Bate	3257
14	8	CARLISLE UNITED	1-2	Carmedy	2737
15	15	York City	0-3		3874
16	22	ROTHERHAM UNITED	0-0		1606
17	Dec 6	BARROW	0-3		2154
18	20	WREXHAM	2-0	Raisbeck, H Robinson(p)	1685
19	25	Hartlepools United	0-4		4518
20	26	HARTLEPOOLS UNITED	1-1	Carmedy	2267
21	27	ROCHDALE	0-0		2774
22	Jan 1	Southport	1-8	Raisbeck	4534
23	3	Darlington	1-2	Raisbeck	2585
24	10	Chesterfield	1-2	Harker	5296
25	17	HALIFAX TOWN	3-2	Harker(p), Martin, Hawes	2462
26	24	New Brighton	0-2		2227
27	31	STOCKPORT COUNTY	1-1	Harker	1593
28	Feb 7	Gateshead	0-2		3161
29	14	DONCASTER ROVERS	2-0	Raisbeck, Harker	2304
30	21	CREWE ALEXANDRA	1-1	Hawes	2232
31	28	Accrington Stanley	1-3	Raisbeck	2216
32	Mar 7	TRANMERE ROVERS	0-4		1546
33	14	Carlisle United	1-8	Harker	3468
34	21	YORK CITY	2-5	Dixon, Raisbeck	1645
35	28	Rotherham United	0-3		3442
36	Apr 3	WIGAN BOROUGH	2-1	Tebb, Raisbeck	1666
37	4	CHESTERFIELD	0-5		1827
38	6	Wigan Borough	1-3	Seabrook (og)	2943
39	11	Barrow	1-2	Carmedy	5307
40	18	SOUTHPORT	1-4	Manoch	1323
41	25	Wrexham	1-5	Tebb	1413
42	May 2	Hull City	0-4		4542

S Walker played in games 31 and 32 at 9

One own goal

F.A. Cup

	Date	Opponent	Score	Scorers	Att
R1	Nov 29	WORKINGTON	4-0	Raidbeck 3, Hawes	2600
R2	Dec 13	YORK CITY	1-1	Allen	3000
rep	18	York City	2-3	H Robinson, Raisbeck	2206

84

NELSON IN FA CUP COMPETITIONS

The year is the final year of the season. The club did not enter in every season

FA CUP

Year	Round	Opponent	H/A	Score
1894	Q1	Bury	H	2-3
1895	Q1	West Manchester	A	6-3
	Q2	Southport Central	A	0-4
1896	PR	Chorley	A	1-3
1897	Q3	Oldham County	H	3-1
	Q4	Newton Heath	A	0-3
1898	Q3	Wigan County	A	1-3
1899	Q3	Southport Central	A	0-3
1900	PR	Trawden Forest	H	2-1
	Q1	Oswaldtwistle Rovers	A	0-3
1901	Q3	Darwen	A	1-3
1902	Q1	Accrington Stanley	A	1-2
1903	Q3	Barrow	H	3-3
	Q3 r	Barrow	A	0-2
1904	PR	Chorley	H	2-2
	PR r	Chorley	A	1-0
	Q1	Rossendale United	H	3-1
	Q2	Accrington Stanley	A	1-2
1905	Q1	Padiham	A	1-0
	Q2	Colne	H	3-1
	Q3	Carlisle Red Rose	H	9-0
	Q4	Darwen	H	1-1
	Q4 r	Darwen	A	3-2
	Q5	Blackpool	A	0-1
1906	PR	Accrington Stanley	A	0-7
1907	PR	Rossendale United	H	2-3
1908	PR	Denton	H	2-1
1908	Q1	Chorley	A	1-3
1909	EP	Halliwell Unitarians	A	4-0
	PR	Bacup	H	7-1
	Q1	Colne	H	2-3
1910	PR	Brierfield Swifts	A	3-2
	Q1	Colne	A	0-1
		Void game - replayed		
	Q1 r	Colne	A	1-1
	Q1 r2	Colne	H	1-2
1911	Q4	Barrow	H	5-0
	Q5	Exeter City	H	3-4
1912	Q1	Haslingden	H	3-2
	Q2	Colne	H	0-2
1913	PR	Leyland	A	6-1
	Q1	Darwen	H	3-1
	Q2	Haslingden	H	2-0
	Q3	Southport Central	H	3-1
	Q4	Halifax Town	A	3-3
	Q4 r	Halifax Town	H	2-3
1914	Q1	Haslingden	A	0-0
	Q1 r	Haslingden	H	2-1
	Q2	Leyland	H	3-1
	Q3	Southport Central	A	0-3
1915	PR	Tottington	H	9-1
	Q1	Chorley	A	0-1
1920	PR	Accrington Stanley	A	2-1
	Q1	Horwich RMI	H	0-1
1921	PR	Skelmersdale United	H	4-1
	Q1	Horwich RMI	H	3-0
	Q2	Fleetwood	A	0-5
1922	Q4	Accrington Stanley	A	1-0
	Q5	Rochdale	H	3-2
	Q6	Worksop Town	A	1-2
1923	Q4	Rochdale	A	1-0
	Q5	Stalybridge Celtic	A	0-1
1924	Q5	Wigan Borough	A	1-1
	Q5 r	Wigan Borough	H	0-1
1925	Q5	Winsford United	H	4-1
	Q6	Coventry City	H	0-1
1926	R1	Wigan Borough	A	0-3
1927	R1	Stockport County	H	4-1
	R2	Ashington	A	1-2
1928	R1	Bradford Park Avenue	H	0-3
1930	R1	Crewe Alexandra	H	0-3
1931	R1	Workington	H	4-0
	R2	York City	H	1-1
	R2 r	York City	A	2-3
1932	Q4	Manchester Central	H	1-3

FA CUP - continued

Year	Round	Opponent	H/A	Score
1933	Q4	Lancaster Town	H	6-0
	R1	Southport	A	3-3
	R1 r	Southport	H	0-4
1935	PR	Breightmet United	H	3-1
	Q1	Wigan Athletic	A	1-3
1936	Q1	Morecambe	A	1-0
	Q2	Dick, Kerrs	A	1-1
	Q2 r	Dick, Kerrs	H	3-4
1937	Q1	Chorley	A	scr
1947	PR	Morecambe	H	1-2
1948	Q1	Chorley	H	2-1
	Q2	Horwich RMI	H	4-1
	Q3	Fleetwood	A	1-1
	Q3 r	Fleetwood	H	2-1
	Q4	Lancaster City	A	1-5
1949	PR	De Havilland (Bolton)	A	1-0
	Q1	Fleetwood	A	0-1
1950	PR	Barnoldswick & District	A	3-1
	Q1	Darwen	A	5-0
	Q2	Fleetwood	A	2-3
1951	Q1	Lancaster City	H	5-2
	Q2	Leyland Motors	H	4-1
	Q3	Dacup Borough	A	2-0
	Q4	Hyde United	A	2-2
	Q4 r	Hyde United	H	3-0
	R1	Witton Albion	A	2-1
	R2	Port Vale	A	2-3
1952	Q4	Skelmersdale United	A	3-0
	R1	Oldham Athletic	H	0-4
1953	Q4	Rhyl	H	1-3
1954	Q4	Winsford United	H	1-0
	R1	Witton Albion	A	1-4
1955	PR	Lytham	H	3-0
	Q1	Leyland Motors	H	8-2
	Q2	Chorley	A	2-4
1956	Q1	Ashton United	A	1-1
	Q1 r	Ashton United	H	1-4
1957	Q1	Chorley	A	1-4
1958	Q1	Chorley	A	1-5
1959	Q1	Bacup Borough	A	3-2
	Q2	Skelmersdale United	A	0-2
1960	PR	Ashton United	H	0-0
	PR r	Ashton United	A	2-1
	Q1	Lytham	H	2-2
	Q1 r	Lytham	A	0-2
1961	Q1	Stalybridge Celtic	H	6-2
	Q2	Bacup Borough	A	2-0
	Q3	Chorley	H	7-4
	Q4	Macclesfield Town	H	2-3
1962	Q1	Leyland Motors	H	4-0
	Q2	Stalybridge Celtic	A	0-1
1963	Q1	Hyde United	A	0-3
1964	Q1	Bacup Borough	H	5-1
	Q2	Chorley	A	1-6
1965	Q1	Lytham	H	2-1
	Q2	Hyde United	A	3-1
	Q3	Stalybridge Celtic	H	2-3
1966	Q1	Chorley	A	0-6
1967	Q1	Lytham	A	1-0
	Q2	Morecambe	H	0-4
1968	Q1	Penrith	A	0-4
1969	PR	Netherfield (Kendal)	N	0-4
2003	EP	Norton & Stockton Anc.	H	0-0
	EP r	Norton & Stockton Anc.	A	2-1
	PR	Bishop Auckland	H	2-3
2004	PR	Witton Albion	A	1-4
2005	EP	Chester-le-Street Town	H	0-1
2006	EP	Retford United	H	2-4
2007	EP	Liversedge	A	0-2
2008	EP	Hallam	A	0-2

FA TROPHY

Year	Round	Opponent	H/A	Score
1973	Q1	Rossendale United	H	0-6
1974	Q1	Worksop Town	H	1-4
1975	PR	Rossendale United	A	0-2
1976	PR	Clitheroe	A	1-0
	Q1	Winterton Rangers	H	5-1
	Q2	Emley	A	1-2
1977	Q1	Accrington Stanley	A	1-5
1978	Q1	Droylsden	A	1-5

FA VASE

Year	Round	Opponent	H/A	Score
1979	PR	Old Blackburnians	H	6-2
	R1	Salford Amateurs	A	1-2
1980	PR	Bradley Rangers	H	0-4
1984	PR	Bradley Rangers	A	1-1
	PR r	Bradley Rangers	H	0-1
1985	PR	Atherton LR	A	3-4
1986	PR	Ford Motors	A	2-1
1986	R1	Kirkby Town	H	1-8
1987	EP	Poulton Victoria	A	0-3
1988	PR	Uniasco	H	1-2
1989	EP	Eppleton CW	H	1-2
1990	EP	Poulton Victoria	A	0-*
1997	Q1	Rossendale United	A	2-0
	Q2	Easington Colliery	H	2-4
2000	Q1	Skelmersdale United	H	0-6
2001	Q2	Liversedge	A	1-2
2002	Q1	Norton & Stockton Anc.	A	2-2
	Q1 r	Norton & Stockton Anc.	H	3-0
	Q2	Garforth Town	H	8-0
	R1	Louth United	A	3-1
	R2	Clitheroe	A	1-1
	R2 r	Clitheroe	H	1-3
2003	Q1	Curzon Ashton	H	2-0
	Q2	Evenwood Town	H	2-1
	R1	Dunston Federation Brwy	A	0-1
2004	Q2	Maine Road	H	3-1
	R1	Squires Gate	A	2-4
2005	Q2	Jarrow Roofing Boldon CA	A	1-5
2006	Q2	Flixton	H	3-2
	R1	Daisy Hill	A	1-0
	R2	Ashville	H	0-1
2007	Q2	Castleton Gabriels	A	6-0
	R1	Sheffield	H	0-1
2008	Q2	Squires Gate	A	2-4

TODAY'S NELSON FC

Many thanks to Gary Broughton, the Nelson club secretary, for these photographs. Please visit the web site at www.nelsonfc.co.uk for the latest news of the club

The 2009-10 squad: Back row, left to right: Stuart Thompson (coach and assistant), Michael Cheetham, Darren Wright, John Luker (captain), Chris Thompson, Alex Mugan (player manager), Daniel Finch, Ashley Higgins, Mark Berry (assistant manager), Chris Ogunyode. Front: Martin Payne, Ashley Williams, Sam Heap, Chris Walker, Phil Prescott, Luke Hargreaves, Lance Ogunyode, Peter Maidment.

Action from the Nelson v Atherton LR game

Action from Nelson v Selby Town

Victoria Park, Nelson

ABOUT THE AUTHOR

Garth Dykes was born at Mellor, near Blackburn, and was educated at Chadderton Grammar School. Qualifications in cotton spinning followed, and a career in yarn sales commenced in 1957, with weekly visits to weavers in Nelson, Colne and Burnley a major part of working life in those far-off days. A career move took Garth to Leicester in 1961 and he retired in 1992 at the age of 58. A member of the Football Writers' Association, Garth's lifelong love of football, which commenced when he attended his first match in season 1945-46, has seen his involvement in twelve books to date. A number of caricatures drawn by the author appear within the pages of this book. This aspect of his work has appeared in several of his earlier titles, as well as in football programmes, national magazines and in several sets of trade cards produced and marketed by David Rowland of Bury.

BY THE SAME AUTHOR

Oldham Athletic – A Complete Record, 1899 -1988 (Breedon Books, 1988)
Exeter City – A Complete Record, 1904–1990, with Alex Wilson and Maurice Golesworthy (Breedon Books 1990)
New Brighton – A Complete Record of the Rakers in the Football League, 1922–1951 (Breedon Books 1990)
Accrington Stanley – A Complete Record, 1894–1962, with Mike Jackman (Breedon Books 1991)
The United Alphabet – A Complete Who's Who of Manchester United F.C. (ACL and Polar Publishing (UK) Ltd. 1994)
All The Lads – A Complete Who's Who of Sunderland A.F.C., with Doug Lamming (Polar Publishing, 1999)
Latics Lads – The Official Who's Who of Oldham Athletic A.F.C., 1907–2002 (Yore Publications, 2002)
Meadow Lane Men – The Complete Who's Who of Notts County F.C., 1888–2005 (Yore Publications, 2005)
The Legends of Oldham Athletic (Breedon Books, 2006)
The Who's Who of Oldham Athletic (Breedon Books, 2008)
A Who's Who of Barrow A.F.C. – Barrow's Football League Players 1921–1972 (Soccerdata, 2009)

Ted Broadhead's medals: on the left, Lancashire Combination winners 1925-26. On the right, Football League Division Three (North) winners, 1922-23.